Mother Teresa

Mother Teresa

Sue Shaw

Marshall Pickering
An Imprint of HarperCollinsPublishers

Marshall Pickering is an Imprint of
HarperCollins*Religious*
Part of HarperCollins*Publishers*
77–85 Fulham Palace Road, London W6 8JB

First published in Great Britain
in 1993 by Marshall Pickering

1 3 5 7 9 10 8 6 4 2

Copyright © 1993 Sue Shaw

Sue Shaw asserts the moral right to be
identified as the author of this work

A catalogue record for this book is
available from the British Library

ISBN 0 551 02713-4

Printed and bound in Great Britain by
HarperCollinsManufacturing Glasgow

CHAPTER ONE

The crowd of angry young men surged forward shouting, "Death to the Mother! Death to the Mother!" Grasping sticks and stones high in the air, they jostled and pushed nearer and nearer to the front of Mother Teresa's "Home for the Dying".

A small midde-aged woman stepped into the sunlight from inside the low, white-washed building. She spoke in a firm but gentle voice. "If this is the way you want it, kill me, I will go straight to heaven. But you must stop this nonsense. You cannot go on like this."

At her words the jeering and shouting stopped. Dropping their weapons, the men looked down shame-faced, unable to hold the gaze of Mother Teresa. One by one they turned to leave. For the time being the danger had passed.

Ever since Mother Teresa had opened the "Home for the Dying" in Calcutta, the local people had been openly hostile and critical. They complained about the steady stream of gaunt, sick people who arrived on stretchers or in ambulances at the Home. No matter how ill they were, they were never turned away. The angry crowd jeered at the funeral processions when corpses, wrapped in white cloths, were carried from the home through the streets.

But Mother Teresa wasn't afraid of opposition. She had no doubt that she had been called by God to serve the poor and that He would protect her.

She had crossed continents to follow Him. She had been born in the city of Skopje, situated in the small kingdom of Serbia, which is part of former Yugoslavia, Eastern Europe. Given the names Agnes Gonxhe Bojaxhiu at her birth on 26th August 1910, Skopje was still part of the Ottoman Empire under the control of Turkish rulers. Agnes's Albanian parents already had two other children, the eldest, Age, a girl, was born in 1904, the second, Lazar, a boy was born in 1907.

Their father, Nikola, was a rich businessman who owned a building company and imported food, cloth and leather from countries as far away as Egypt. His business meant he travelled overseas regularly, and his children looked forward to the special presents he would bring back with him from his travels. He was a loving and generous father and took great interest in his children's education.

His wife, Drana, was deeply involved in the Church and was always busy. She kept their spacious house and fruit-tree-filled garden running efficiently and always found time to help others.

Although Agnes was her first name her family called her Gonxha. Her brother Lazar explained: "'Gonxha' means a flower bud in Albanian, and we thought of her as a little rosebud. When she was a child, she was plump, round and tidy. She was sensible and a little too serious for her age. Of the three of us, she was the one who did not steal the jam. However, being generous and kindhearted, she would help me in the dining room to pull open the drawer of the cupboard high up against the wall because I could not manage it myself."

Lazar's weakness for jam led to midnight raids, when he helped himself to anything sweet that was in the kitchen cupboard. When he was older, Agnes, hearing him making a noise, would creep downstairs and remind him not to eat after midnight if they were going to communion with their mother in the morning. But she never told on him.

Agnes wasn't always serious and sensible. One evening the children were talking together about lots of silly things, and as time went on their talk became sillier and sillier. Their mother sat listening but said nothing. Eventually she left the room and turned off the main electric switch, plunging the house into total darkness. "She told us", says Mother Teresa, "that there was no use wasting electricity so that such foolishness could go on." Mother Teresa never forgot that particular incident and throughout her life has avoided foolish talk and waste of any kind.

Both her parents were determined to keep their Christian faith even though they were greatly outnumbered by the many Muslims living around them. Both Nikola and Drana had a great influence on Agnes. Her father, a caring member of the local community, helped to build Skopje's first theatre, sat on the town council and gave generously to the Church and the poor. Before leaving on a business trip, he always left enough money with his wife so that she would be ready to give to anyone who came to the door asking for help. Their door was always open to any in need.

The memory of her family's sharing always stayed with Agnes. She later remembered, "Many of the poor in and around Skopje knew our house, and none left it empty-handed. We had guests at table every day. At first I used to ask 'Who are they?', and mother would say, 'Some are relatives but all of them are our people'. When I was older, I realized that the strangers were poor people who had nothing and whom my mother was feeding."

One time, when Drana found a woman alone and uncared for, in agony with a painful tumour, she brought her into their home until she was fully recovered. Drana also went regularly with food and money to visit the poor, and although she was still very young Agnes accompanied her.

One of their father's special interests was campaigning for the creation of Albania, a land Albanian people could call their own. He joined in political discussions and attended meetings whenever they concerned Albania. One day in 1919, when Agnes was nine years old, he left Skopje to travel one hundred and sixty miles to Belgrade where he was invited to a political dinner. He left home a healthy man of forty-five but came home a dying man.

Drana sent Agnes hurrying to the nearby church to fetch the priest, but he was not there. Agnes thought he might be leaving for a trip or coming back, so she ran down to the railway station in the hope of meeting him. There was a priest on the platform but she did not recognize him. Plucking up courage she approached him and explained about her desperately ill father.

The priest rushed back with her to pray quietly with her father, preparing him for death, and then left. They never saw him again. Nikola was rushed to the local hospital for emergency surgery but it was unsuccessful. The doctors and the family were convinced he had been poisoned by his opponents.

Nikola's unexpected death meant Agnes's mother, Drana, had to bring up the three children alone. She could not continue her husband's business, so she used her needlework skills to make fine clothes, and sold locally hand-crafted carpets and various types of cloth.

Although her family was no longer wealthy, Drana continued to follow her husband's example, giving meals and help to the poor and old. The home was open to any friends of the children, some of whom came to ask Agnes for help with their schoolwork. In secondary school Agnes was always top of the class and she was very popular, especially with the girls.

The whole family was musical, singing, playing instruments and putting on concerts at home. Agnes and Age belonged to the church choir and took part in charity concerts and plays. Both girls had unusual singing voices and were nicknamed "the Nightingales" of the choir. Every evening the family prayed together and joined in all the various activities of the church.

Their priest, Father Jambrenkovic, loved working with young people, and he started a library where they could borrow great works of literature by authors like the Russian novelist Dostoevksy. Agnes spent hours reading. Whenever she had some spare time she buried her nose in a good book.

Agnes also enjoyed writing and carried a notebook around with her in case she felt inspired to jot something down. From time to time she would read to her friends some poetry she had written. Two articles she wrote were published in the local newspaper, *Blagovest*. Those who knew her well thought she had the talent to be a writer.

Father Jambrenkovic also started a society

for young Catholics which organized walks, outings, lectures and meetings, and Agnes soon became an enthusiastic member. The priest encouraged them to pray in small groups for missionary work around the world, and provided them with a missionary magazine.

He also introduced them to the lives of saints and missionaries, and challenged them to think about some words of Saint Ignatius Loyola – "What have I done for Christ? What am I doing for Christ? What will I do for Christ?" By the time Agnes was fourteen she had heard enough to know she wanted to work for Christ as a missionary.

About this time, some Yugoslav priests had gone to work in Calcutta, India. The first group arrived there in 1924 and some of them were sent to Kurseong in the far north-east of India, some to the outskirts of Calcutta. They wrote long, exciting letters about their adventures, which Father Jambrenkovic read regularly to the group. Young Agnes was inspired and her fascination with India burst into life.

Along with two other girls in the group, Agnes was taking mandolin lessons from her cousin, Lorenc, who never asked for any payment. However Agnes urged him to take a dinar from each girl for each lesson. "Take it," she insisted, "and give it to me for the missions in India."

Full of enthusiasm and hope, Agnes wrote to the priests asking if there were any religious sisters serving in the same area. "I wanted to be a missionary", she said later. "I wanted to go out and give the life of Christ to the people." The Yugoslav Brothers wrote back to say the Sisters of Loreto had been working there for over seventy years amongst the poor and needy.

The Sisters were an international order of nuns founded in 1609 by a Yorkshire woman, Mary Ward. Unlike other nuns, they did not live shut away from the outside world but obtained special permission from the Church to go out and work among the poor. Those who served in India began their training in Dublin, Ireland. Agnes was thrilled at the news of the Loreto Sisters and began to pray about joining the order herself.

For Agnes, becoming a Loreto nun would mean leaving her home, her family and her country. As travel was so time-consuming and no one had holidays, it was very likely that she would never see her family or friends again. While she was trying to decide what to do, Agnes asked her cousin Antoni for advice.

"How do you know if God is calling you?" she enquired.

"Father Jambrenkovic says," he replied, "when you think God is calling you, you should feel a great joy about serving Him and your neighbour." Spreading his arms out wide he continued, "Father says this joy should be like a compass showing you the direction in which to go."

Eventually Agnes told her mother she had decided to become a missionary. Knowing she would never see her daughter again Drana returned to her room, where she stayed for twenty-four hours. Maybe she prayed. Maybe she cried. Agnes never knew. When Drana came out she spoke some words that her daughter has always treasured "Put your hand in His – in His hand – and walk all the way with Him."

When Lazar, away serving in the army, heard the news of his little sister's decision he was shocked. He wrote to her: "I want to know, how can a lovely young girl give up a good life and go so far away, probably never to see me or the family again?" Agnes replied and wrote some words that Lazar never forgot. "You will serve a King of two million people. I shall serve the King of the whole world. Which of us do you think is in the better place?"

So, at the age of eighteen, Agnes prepared for a totally unknown future. Her young friends from church organized a farewell concert, and the evening before she left they brought gifts to her home. Next morning about one hundred people gathered at the railway station to wave goodbye to Agnes, who was to be accompanied by her mother and sister as far as the city of Zagreb. Waving her handkerchief to her friends as the train moved out of the station, Agnes wept.

In Zagreb, they met up with another young woman, Betike Kanjc, who also wanted to join the Loreto nuns. At the main station Drana and Age watched Agnes, their little "Rosebud" and the youngest of the family, board a train that was to take her out of their lives for ever.

For two young women to be travelling alone across Europe in 1929 was a daring adventure. The first part of the journey took them through Austria, Germany and France. Arriving in Paris, the girls were interviewed by the Sister in charge of the Loreto nuns there. With the help of an interpreter from the Yugoslavian Embassy, she discovered that both girls wanted to work in India. On the Sister's recommendation, the Head of the Order gave the girls the permission they needed to leave for Dublin.

A few days later the girls arrived in Dublin where they began an intensive course studying English, their tutor being a nun who had spent many years working in India. After only six weeks they embarked on the next stage of their missionary journey, the long voyage to India. With them on the ship were three Franciscan nuns with whom they met to pray. The ship, often rolling and tossing in heavy seas, took them through the Suez Canal, the Red Sea, the vast Indian Ocean and finally into the Bay of Bengal.

En route they stopped briefly in Colombo, the capital city of Ceylon (now Sri Lanka), where Agnes was first exposed to poverty. She recorded her thoughts in a letter . . . "we were shocked to the depths of our beings by the indescribable poverty. Many families live along the streets, along the city walls, even in places thronged by people. Day and night they live in the open on mats they have made from large palm leaves – or often on the bare ground. They are all virtually naked, wearing at best a ragged loincloth."

After seven weeks at sea they arrived in Calcutta in the first week of January 1929. No sooner had she arrived than Agnes was sent one hundred and fifty miles north to a convent at Darjeeling, a mountain resort at the foot of the mighty Himalayas, where she joined other girls who were preparing to become nuns.

Their days were spent studying the Bible, learning English and training to be teachers, which involved two hours' teaching practice every morning with some local children in a one-roomed school. They were also introduced to two Indian languages, Hindi and Bengali, and studied the lives of saints, one of whom, Saint Therese, greatly impressed Agnes.

Saint Therese had persuaded the authorities to let her become a nun at the age of fifteen. Her love for missionary work and prayer made a big impact on all those who knew her. She chose to serve the poor in Hanoi, Vietnam, then a colony of France, where she died tragically from tuberculosis at the young age of twenty-four.

Saint Therese believed that small, everyday acts of service and kindness were far more important than religious experiences. She once wrote, "My little way . . . is the way of trust and absolute self-surrender."

Agnes, deeply moved by these words and by her life, decided to take as her name in religious life that of Saint Therese. Her name was to be spelt in the Spanish way as there already was a Sister Therese in the order. So on 24th May 1931 Agnes made her first vows of poverty, chastity and obedience, leaving behind the name she was given at birth and becoming Sister Teresa.

Sister Teresa now took the train back down to Calcutta to begin work. Leaving behind the cool, mountain air and the sweet-smelling meadows, she arrived in a steamy, hot and crowded city. Calcutta, once known as the City of Palaces because of its ornate and opulent buildings set in spacious gardens, was also called Nightmare City. It grew without plan, attracting rich and poor alike. The poor flocked to the city in the hope of finding work, the rich came to make money. Great wealth and splendour existed side by side with filth and squalor.

Sister Teresa was now qualified to teach and was sent to St Mary's school in the east of Calcutta, which stood in the well-kept grounds of the Loreto Convent. St Mary's had about two hundred pupils, girls who came from a variety of different backgrounds. Some came from middle-class families, some from poorer families, others were orphans. Using her newly-learnt Bengali,

Sister Teresa began teaching the girls Geography and later History. Looking back on this time in her life, Mother Teresa said, "Loreto meant everything to me. I loved teaching."

Her day began before dawn when she spent time praying and reading the Bible and other religious works. Before the busyness of teaching began she attended Communion in the school chapel, and after a long school day returned to the chapel for evening prayer. Day after day Sister Teresa kept this routine, beginning and ending the day in prayer no matter how much work had to be accomplished.

For the next nineteen years Sister Teresa followed this demanding schedule, but she never complained. "When I was eighteen I decided to leave my home and become a nun. Since then I have never doubted, even for a second, that I did the right thing. It was the will of God, His choice." On 14th May 1937 she took her lifetime vows of poverty, chastity and obedience. She was now a professed nun.

In time, Sister Teresa became the headmistress of St Mary's. She was also given responsibility for an order of Bengali nuns, the Daughters of Saint Anne, who taught in the local Bengali High School.

Some of the girls at St Mary's, like Sister Teresa when she was a teenager, belonged to a religious society which arranged discussions, prayers and study. Father Julien Henry, pastor of the local church, ran this group and invited the girls to talk about how they could help the many poor families who lived in a nearby slum area called Mohti Jihl. The slum had grown up around a pond which was now polluted and discoloured.

Keen to be involved, the girls went out in groups every Saturday, visiting families who lived in mud-floored huts, and fetching water for them from the dirty pond. Other groups talked to patients at a local hospital and brought them small gifts. But Sister Teresa, because of her vows, was unable to join them although she was delighted to know the girls wanted to serve others.

During the years that Sister Teresa taught at St Mary's, India was struggling to break free from British domination. Mahatma Gandhi was inspiring millions of ordinary Indians to resist their unwelcome masters peacefully.

When, in 1939, the British drew India un-willingly into the Second World War, their need for transport deprived the farmers of the boats which ferried rice from their fields to their customers. Without boats, the rice never reached the people, and at least two million starved to death. Eventually the convent itself felt the effects of the war.

The British were fighting the Japanese in neighbouring Burma (now Myanmar), and took over the convent and school for use as a military hospital. Many of the pupils were evacuated to convents and hotels miles away, while those remaining moved to a building on nearby Convent Road. Sister Teresa took charge of this building, continuing to teach and supervise the Daughters of St Anne.

In 1946, another tragedy struck Calcutta. Although Britain had agreed to hand over power to the Indian people, the two major religious groups, Muslims and Hindus, could not agree on a new government and threatened to disrupt the negotiations. After a mass meeting of Muslims on 16th August in the Maidan, Calcutta's central park, violence broke out. Shops were set alight, people fled in all directions. Traffic came to a standstill. Deliveries of food and supplies stopped. As headmistress of the school Sister Teresa had to take action.

"I went out from St Mary's. I had three hundred girls in the boarding school and we had nothing to eat. We were not supposed to go out into the streets, but I went anyway. Then I saw the bodies on the street, stabbed, beaten, lying there in pools of dried blood.

"We had been behind our safe walls. We knew there had been rioting. People had been jumping over our walls, first a Hindu, then a Muslim. A lorry full of soldiers stopped me and told me I should not be out. I told them I had to come out and take the risk. I had three hundred students and nothing to eat. The soldiers had rice and they drove me back to the school and unloaded bags of rice."

That day five thousand people died and fifteen thousand were wounded, and it was for ever remembered as The Day of the Great Killing. It was the first time in many years that Sister Teresa had ventured beyond the walls of her school. Yet less than one month after the tragedy, God spoke to Sister Teresa in such an unmistakable way, that she knew she had to leave Loreto and return to those blood-stained streets.

CHAPTER TWO

Shortly after her experience of Calcutta's streets, Sister Teresa left the city on her annual visit to the convent at Darjeeling, where she spent time in prayer and study. Her train journey north was booked for 10th September 1946, a day which is now celebrated by her followers as "Inspiration Day" as a result of what happened.

"It was on that train that I heard the call to give up all and follow Him into the slums – to serve Him among the poorest of the poor. I knew it was His will and that I had to follow Him. There was no doubt it was to be His work. The message was quite clear. I was to leave the convent and work with the poor while living among them. It was an order. I knew where I belonged, but I did not know how to get there."

Sister Teresa heard God's call for the second time. Years earlier she had heard His call to leave the world to be a nun for life. Now she had received a second call, to leave her religious order to serve the poor. But before she could think of leaving, she needed to persuade the church authorities that God really was speaking to her.

On her return from Darjeeling, Sister Teresa wrote to Father Celeste Van Exem, who for many years had helped her to understand what God was doing in her life. She described how she believed God had given her a new mission. Father Celeste advised Sister Teresa to keep her thoughts secret, and promised to talk fully with Archbishop Perier, Archbishop of Calcutta.

When the Bishop first heard the news he was very concerned at the idea of a lone nun on Calcutta's streets and wondered how the school would be affected, so he recommended that Sister Teresa wait one whole year before making any decisions. She was not surprised by his caution, "I did not expect any other reply. An Archbishop cannot allow a nun to found a new Order at the drop of a hat, as if she alone had some sort of unique message from God."

For India that year, 1947, was also a year of traumatic change. It was the year when India became independent of Britain, and new borders were drawn to create West Pakistan (now Pakistan) and East Pakistan (now Bangladesh). Fanatical Muslim leaders encouraged their followers to use violence to prove that Hindus and Muslims could not live peacefully together in a free India. The fighting spread all over India, forcing thousands to flee for their lives.

Muslims flocked into two parts of the newly created Pakistan, Hindus and Sikhs into India. Four million Hindus took refuge in the state of Bengal, swelling the already crowded city of Calcutta. Sister Teresa could only watch and pray.

At the end of the year, Archbishop Perier gave Sister Teresa permision to write to the head of her Order asking to be allowed to leave "in order to spend herself in the service of the poor and the needy in the slums of Calcutta, and to gather around her some companions ready to undertake the same work."

Writing her letter first in rough, she asked if she could continue her vows as a nun but work in a new area amongst the poor. However, the Archbishop felt Sister Teresa should no longer be a nun and he insisted that she change her letter and ask to be freed from her vows as a nun.

Sister Teresa dutifully rewrote the letter and sent it to the head of her Order back in Ireland, who replied that she was happy for Sister Teresa to leave the convent on condition she had permission from the Pope in Rome. Another letter was drafted to the Pope, and again Archbishop Perier insisted that Sister Teresa must ask to be freed from her vows as a nun.

With the help of Father Celeste, Sister Teresa wrote that God was calling her to give up all to serve the poorest of the poor in the slums. The letter was sent, in February 1948, to one of the Pope's ambassadors living in Delhi, who would forward it to Rome.

March, April, May, June and most of July went by without any reply. At the end of July the Archbishop called Father Celeste into his office and announced, "She has it". Not only had she permission to leave the convent but she was also allowed to remain a nun. The very thing Sister Teresa had prayed for but been unable to ask for, she had been granted.

A few days later, when Father Celeste told Sister Teresa he had the reply she had been waiting for, she turned pale and said she wanted to go to the chapel to pray. On her return he gave her the news she had longed to hear. "Can I go to the slums now?" she asked, her brown eyes sparkling with excitement. "It's not as simple as that. First we have to tell the head of the convent, the rest of the Sisters, and the girls."

The news came as a real shock for many who knew Sister Teresa. Some wept. For Sister Teresa herself it was an emotional time. "To leave Loreto was my greatest sacrifice, the most difficult thing I have ever done. It was much more difficult than to leave my family and country to enter religious life", she recollected. The arrangement was that Sister Teresa should leave the convent for a year, after which time she would return if her work had not been successful. Instead of reporting to the head of the Order she now had to report to the Archbishop of Calcutta.

On 16th August 1948 Sister Teresa said her brief final farewell to Father Celeste. She wanted to slip away unnoticed, particularly as she had replaced her traditional black habit with the plain cotton white sari, worn by the local poor women.

She now looked like an ordinary Indian woman, except that her sari was wrapped around her head over a tiny cotton cap, and a small black crucifix was attached to her left shoulder with a safety pin.

Two years had passed since first hearing her call to the poor. But what had seemed impossible God had made possible! She was almost thirty-eight years old.

On Father Celeste's advice she was heading first to Patna, 385 kilometres (240 miles) from Calcutta, where she would learn some nursing skills from medical missionary nuns who ran a hospital and outpatients department for the city's poor.

After a warm welcome from the Sisters she was quickly introduced to the harsh realities of working with the sick. She was expected to help with emergencies, operations and births, and soon learnt to care for abandoned babies, to comfort patients with fatal diseases like cholera and smallpox, and to cope with gruesome accidents.

One of the doctors recalled "I remember nothing fazed her. She just wanted to know what was going on and what she could do to help." The Director of the Nursing School, Mother Dengal, made sure Sister Teresa learnt as much as possible. "As she had never had any nursing before, I taught her simple procedures, making a hospital bed, giving injections and medications."

When Sister Teresa announced, "My Sisters and I will eat only rice and salt", Mother Dengal disagreed strongly. "Do you want to help the poor and the sick or do you want to die with them?" she demanded. "Do you want your young nuns to lose their lives, or do you want them healthy and strong, so they can work for Christ?" Sister Teresa quickly admitted her error and heeded the advice.

The course completed, in December 1948 Sister Teresa boarded the train for her return to Calcutt, hugging a pair of sturdy sandals, a gift from the Sisters. Arriving on the streets of Calcutta with five rupees (about 30p) and little else, she discovered the city streets were filled with refugees, mainly Hindus who had fled from the new Muslim-controlled East Pakistan. When they arrived in Calcutta they simply camped out wherever they could find a space.

Father Van Exem had arranged for her to stay with an Order of nuns, The Little Sisters of the Poor, who cared for the elderly. For the first few days Sister Teresa helped the nuns with their work, spending her mornings praying alone.

On 21st December she decided to start her own work in Mohti Jihl, the slum area where some of her former pupils had visited poor families. It was about an hour's walk from the old people's home. Finding a space between some huts, she asked a workman who was doing nothing to dig away the grass so she could set up an open-air school.

"After I had talked with the mothers and fathers and asked if they wanted their children to learn, they sent them to me", Mother Teresa later explained. "The first day I had just a few children, perhaps five. I sat on a chair under a tree and the children gathered round me on the ground. I had no money for slates or chalk or a blackboard, so when they came to write something, I took a stick to mark it on the ground where the children were sitting. I began with teaching them the alphabet because, although they were all big children, they had never been to school and no school wanted them. Then we had practical lessons on hygiene. I told them how to wash themselves . . . They were such good children. They wanted to learn."

Each day she returned and the number of children grew rapidly. To encourage good attendance and cleanliness Sister Teresa gave out bars of soap as prizes. As well as reading and writing she taught the children how to keep as clean as possible with the small amount of water they had.

At first Sister Teresa worked all alone. She was an unusual sight, a European woman wearing a rough cotton sari, with bare feet in plain sandals. To show her commitment to the new independent nation of India, she applied to become an Indian citizen. Some who knew her well found her way of life hard to understand. "We thought she was cracked", one priest admitted.

Some days Sister Teresa herself needed to ask God to help her to keep going. One day she wrote in her diary: "God wants me to be a lonely nun, laden with the poverty of the cross. Today I learnt a good lesson. The poverty of the poor is so hard. When I was going and going till my legs and arms were paining, I was thinking how they have to suffer to get food and shelter. Then the comfort of Loreto came to tempt me, but out of my own free choice, my God, and out of love for You, I desire to remain and do whatever is Your holy will for me. Give me courage now, this moment."

When Sister Teresa decided she needed a place of her own to stay, Father Van Exem introduced her to a member of a Bengali Catholic family, Michael Gomes, who offered her an empty room on the second floor of his large home, at 14 Creek Lane. In February 1949 she moved in, bringing a suitcase, a packing case to act as a desk, a chair and some wooden boxes to serve as seats.

On her first day she had a visitor. Chaura Ma, meaning "the mother of Chaura", was an old Bengali widow who used to work at th Loreto Convent as a cook. Being very fond of Sister Teresa she had decided to leave her job to stay and help.

As news spread about the school, people began to send small gifts which enabled Chaura Ma and Sister Teresa to shop for supplies. Someone donated a table, then a chair, later a cupboard for the school.

Then on 19th March a young girl appeared at 14 Creek Lane. She was Subashini Bas, the nineteen-year-old daughter of a wealthy Bengali family who had been a pupil at St Mary's School since she was nine. On discovering that her former headmistress was working in the slums of Calcutta, she had decided to join her. Like Sister Teresa, she wanted to surrender herself to God and serve the poorest of the poor.

A few weeks later another student from St Mary's, Magdalena Gomes, arrived and announced that she too was determined to give all to God and share in the work. By Easter there were three young women working in Mohti Jihl, and within a few months ten, all from St Mary's, had joined Sister Teresa.

To accommodate them all, Michael Gomes offered them a large attic room in the same house. From here the young women, all dressed in plain cotton saris, went out to the slums. Sister Teresa arranged their day so that some of the girls had time to continue studying for various exams, and if necesary she gave them extra tuition.

By 5.30 a.m. they were praying in the local church, where Sister Teresa's old friend, Father Henry, was priest. By 7.30 they were out on the streets. Remembering the lessons she learnt at Patna, Sister Teresa made sure they ate plenty of cheap but nourishing chappatis before they left.

Father Van Exem, seeing that they needed

more resources, placed an advertisement in the respected *Calcutta Statesman* describing the Sisters' work in the slums. To his surprise, the first gift of a hundred rupees came from the Chief Minister of Bengal, and the newspaper carried further reports of Sister Teresa's work which also brought in gifts of money.

The need to do more than work in the slums became urgent as the Sisters crossed the city, and passed hundreds of people lying in alleys and gutters, close to death. Unable to pick themselves up for lack of strength or burning fever, many died where they lay, until the council workmen carried their bodies away for burial. Many had lived on the streets most of their lives, begging for food or money. Some found themselves there because of debt, unemployment or crippling diseases like leprosy.

To Hindus, the idea of touching a dying body is deeply offensive. If a destitute man were to die in a rented room, the owner would have to paint it to remove the pollution. The poor man might be carried outside at the first sign of death. This fear of being polluted meant countless people were left to die alone. Only those who belonged to the lowest classes of society were permitted to handle a corpse.

Sister Teresa remembered finding one woman lying on the pavement outside one of Calcutta's busiest hospitals. "She had been half-eaten by the rats and ants. I took her to the hospital but they could not do anything for her. They only took her because I refused to move until they accepted her."

There were many other occasions when Sister Teresa tried to persuade hospitals to admit the dying. Transporting patients by taxis and rickshaws, she sometimes had to bargain with the driver who was reluctant to have a passenger near to death. If all else failed she would borrow a wheelbarrow and push the suffering man or woman to hospital.

Many times she was turned away, so she would go from hospital to hospital. Sometimes there was simply no more space, sometimes a real fear that the dying person would infect other patients. Sometimes the hospital just refused to accept someone who could not afford to pay for treatment.

These experiences convinced Sister Teresa that she must do something herself for those dying on the streets of Calcutta. "We cannot let a child of God die like an animal in the gutter", she declared. For a few rupees a week she rented a room in Mohti Jihl where she brought human bodies, near skeletons covered in filthy rags, to spend their last few hours on earth.

Soon two rooms were filled with the dying. Sister Teresa and the young women began to pray for a building of their own. The need was so desperate Sister Teresa went to see the Health Officer of Calcutta, Dr Ahmed. "It is a shame for people to die on our city roads", she told him.

To have a young, educated woman offering to help society's rejects was a staggering proposal but one that Dr Ahmed took seriously. He offered a building next to the temple of Kali, the Hindu goddess of death and destruction. There were two large rooms, electricity and gas connections, and an open courtyard where patients could enjoy the fresh air, and where clothes and bedding could be hung to dry.

It was perfect. Sister Teresa accepted and immediately a squad of girls moved in to clear away the filth of the previous occupants, who were squatters. Seven days later, it was clean enough to move patients there from Mohti Jihl. Sister Teresa named the home "Nimral Hriday". Bengali for "The Place of the Pure Heart", and promised that it would only be used for those who had been rejected by the city's hospitals.

Ambulances began arriving to deliver those no one else wanted. It quickly became known by the police and the health authorities, who sent people there as a last resort.

A few days after the official opening of Nimral Hriday, or Kalighat as it came to be called, Sister Teresa had to report to the Archbishop of Calcutta. A whole year had passed since she had left the convent. There was no doubt that her work must continue and as over ten women were now working with Sister Teresa, they were large enough to become a new Order of nuns.

The Archbishop offered to speak to the Pope personally, and invited Sister Teresa to produce a document describing the principles of her work which he would present to the Pope. Sister Teresa wrote out the usual three vows of poverty, chastity and obedience, and added another even stricter vow that all members had to observe: "to give wholehearted and free service to the poorest of the poor."

Her Order was to be called The Missionaries of Charity, and Sister Teresa was to become Mother Teresa, founder of the Order. On 7th October 1950 the Church gave permission for her new Order to work amongst the poor, the abandoned, the dying, the sick and the lost of Calcutta.

Soon many more young women offered themselves for service. Their contribution to the welfare of the poor in Calcutta was distinctively different from that of government employees. A high government official said, "You and we do the same social work. But the difference between you and us is one we cannot pass over. You work for somebody and we work for something." He knew that somebody was Jesus.

Mother Teresa had very clear ideas about the kind of person needed to join her Order. "The first quality I looked for was joy," she recalled, "my Sisters have to be cheerful. It's no good having people who are easily depressed as there is enough depression on the streets of Calcutta.

I needed people who would bring hope."

Within two years the number of Sisters, many of whom came from wealthy backgrounds, had grown to twenty-eight. In joining they chose to become as poor as the people they served, a lifestyle very different from the one they had known. Each Sister owned two saris, one pair of sandals, a rope girdle, a crucifix, a mattress and a shiny metal bucket for washing herself and her clothes.

"Our rigorous poverty is our safeguard," says Mother Teresa ". . . In order to understand and help those who have nothing, we must live like them . . . The only difference is that these people are poor by birth, and we are poor by choice."

As they were outgrowing the room at 14 Creek Road, Father Van Exem and Father Henry went out on their bikes in search of a larger house.

At that time, many Muslims were leaving Calcutta to escape the increasing hostility between different religious groups. One such person, a magistrate, Mr Islam, had reluctantly decided to migrate to East Pakistan and he needed to sell his large city house. Mr Islam, a Muslim who had been educated by Catholics, was one of Father Van Exem's friends, and when he heard about the need for a building he told he priest, "I got that house from God. I give it back to Him." He willingly agreed to sell the property for £7,500, which only covered the value of the land.

The cost was paid for by the Archbishop, on behalf of the Church in Calcutta.

Father Henry took Mother Teresa to see the property. "Father, it is too big; what to do with all that!" she exclaimed. But Father Henry replied, "Mother, you will need it all. There will be a day when you will ask where to put all your people." In the years to come he was proved right.

Mother Teresa and her Sisters moved into the house on 54A Lower Circular Road in February 1953, and immediately turned one of the rooms into a chapel. Outside, the busy roads were clogged with traffic and the noise of streetsellers and clattering tramcars filled the air, unaware of the serenity and peace behind the walls of the Missionaries of Charity House.

Two months later Mother Teresa accompanied the young women to the Cathedral, where the four Sisters made their first vows as nuns and Mother Teresa restated the final vows she had made in Loreto. As a tribute to Mother Teresa, Subashini took Mother's original name, Agnes, as her religious name.

The scene was set. Over the following months and years the work of the Missionaries of Charity spread throughout Calcutta and beyond, taking the good news that God really does care for the weak and lost.

CHAPTER THREE

Kalighat, the home for the dying, had no doors and was always open. Young and old, men and women, Hindus, Christians, Muslims, atheists alike spent their last days on earth cared for by Mother Teresa and her Sisters.

During the first five years they received more than eight thousand people. "At first," Mother Teresa said, "most died, no matter what we did. Then in 1955 and 1956 about half lived. By 1957 more lived than died."

The two wards, one for men, the other for women, were dimly lit by windows set high in the walls. The nuns wove silently between the rows of camp beds to attend lovingly to every need. Some patients needed open wounds to be cleaned of maggots which bred on rotting flesh. Some had growths that needed to be covered, or stumps where feet and hands had been deformed by leprosy. Others were hardly more than skeletons, their skin stretched taut across ribs which seemed to be struggling to break through.

All nationalities were represented, Nepali, Chinese, Anglo-Indians and British, yet they all shared one common identity of being close to death. For Mother and her Sisters these scraps of humanity were of infinite value. Mother Teresa described them, "These are our treasures. They are Jesus. Each one is Jesus in his distressing disguise. He has told us He is the naked one. He is the thirsty one. He is the one without a home. He is the one who is suffering."

Sadly, during the first few months of its existence, different groups demonstrated their opposition to the home. As it was so near to the Hindu temple of Kali, some Hindus feared that the dying brought pollution too close to their sacred shrine. The temple priests sent letters of complaint to the Calcutta Corporation asking them to evict the Sisters.

The trouble subsided after Mother Teresa helped a temple priest. One day she saw a crowd on the pavement outside the Kali temple surrounding a man who was dying in a pool of mess. No one would touch him because he was in the last stages of tuberculosis, a highly infectious disease. Mother Teresa picked him up and carried him into the home, where she nursed and cared for him.

Mother Teresa tells the story herself, "We had one of the priests from the temple who died here very beautifully. He was so bitter when he came in, very bitter and he was very young, only twenty-four or twenty-five. He was the head priest, I think. No hospital would take him in. He was thrown out. This is why he was so bitter.

He did not want to die when he came, but he changed. He became peaceful and quiet. He was with us only two weeks and people from the temple used to come and visit him every day. They could not believe the change in him."

When the temple priests realized that one of their kind had received so much love and care and had been able to die in peace and with dignity, they accepted that the Missionaries of Charity were trying to help anyone, whatever their religion, and troubled them no more.

Another group, students, fearing that the Sisters were trying to force people to become Christians before they died, went to the Police Commissioner and demanded that he close the home. The Commissioner agreed but said he must first visit it to see things for himself.

The day he arrived, Mother Teresa was attending to a patient who needed treatment for a sore infected by maggots. The repulsive smell was overpowering. Mother Teresa offered to show the Commissioner around but he said he would find his own way.

Meanwhile some of the students came inside the home and gathered around to watch Mother Teresa. When the Commissioner returned and saw them he said, "I have given my word that I will push this lady out and I will keep it. But before I do, you must get your mothers and your sisters to do the work she is doing. Only then will I exercise my authority." Speechless and stunned, they left and never came back.

In nursing the dying, Mother Teresa and her Sisters hoped many would discover God for themselves, but they had no intention of pressurizing people to accept their beliefs. Mother Teresa explained: "What we are trying to do by our work, by serving the people, is to come closer to God . . . I want very much people to come to know God, to love Him, to serve Him, for that is true happiness. And what I have I want everyone in the world to have. But it is their choice. I can only give the means. If I breathe into Kalighat and do some work there and really serve the people with great love and sacrifice, then naturally they will begin to think of God."

For many, Kalighat was the first place where they had ever felt love and acceptance. Charubala was a "child widow". Before her tenth birthday her parents arranged a marriage for her to an older man, but when she reached ten, her husband-to-be died and her relatives, suspecting that Charubula brought bad luck, forced her to work in their homes, treating her harshly.

Eventually Charubula could stand their cruelty no longer, and simply walked out. Alone in Calcutta, she scrounged jobs washing dishes and doing housework. Tragically she contracted an illness which left her with paralysed legs, and she was left to die on the streets.

At Kalighat the nuns washed and combed her hair, and cleaned her lifeless limbs, chatting as they worked. The wonderful sensation of being cared for brought a joy to Charubula that shone from her face. She sang to the other patients and helped to feed those unable to fend for themselves. For the first time in her life, she felt loved and precious.

Charubula's story can be echoed by thousands of others, who have spent most of their lives feeling unwanted and unloved.

The work of Kalighat also affected those who volunteered to help. Students from a local Catholic college helped the Sisters in all aspects of the work. One of the first volunteers was Rama Coomaraswamy, a philosophy student who was expected to follow in the footsteps of his father, who worked for the Museum of Fine Arts in Boston.

"We did what needed to be done to help the Sisters", Rama recalled. "Sometimes we bathed the men as they were brought in from the streets, washing off the filth and maybe the maggots. I remember shaving them and giving them haircuts, even cutting their fingernails and toenails. We often had to sit down and feed a starving man slowly and patiently so he would not die. But they did die. Then it was our job to carry them from the hall into the side space where the corpses were kept.

"The ones who survived found that they

mattered. They seemed surprised to be treated as human beings, that someone took time to serve them and feed them. It only took a few days for them to look human again." When Rama returned to the States he changed the expected course of his life and chose to study medicine, working in New York's vast city hospital, Bellevue, a hospital that always welcomed the city's poorest.

Rama's experience of working at Kalighat had taught him a truth that was close to Mother Teresa's heart, that the poor deserve so much more than they receive. "I believe the people of today do not think that the poor are like them as human beings", says Mother Teresa. "They look down on them. But if they had that deep respect for the dignity of poor people, I am sure it would be easy for them to come closer to them, and to see they, too, are children of God, and that they have a right to the things of life and of love and of service as anybody else.

"In these times of development everybody is in a hurry and everybody's in a rush, and on the way there are people falling down, who are not able to compete. These are the ones we want to love and serve and take care of."

The arrival at the home of a dying young mother led Mother Teresa to start another vital service, rescuing children. The mother, racked by fever and the pains of hunger, was bro into Kalighat clutching her tiny three-year-old child, Usha, whose pitifully thin body was covered with sores.

When Usha's mother died, Mother Teresa told people she was looking for another home to care for children like Usha. Shortly afterwards an old Muslim came to the Missionaries of Charity home and told a Sister that a large house was available for rent a few minutes' walk away. The old man left, never to be seen again, but when investigations were made about the house they proved to be true.

Straightaway Mother Teresa rented the house and named it "Shishu Bhavan", "The Children's Home", and Usha became the first of thousands to be saved from death. The home, a plain two-storeyed building with a large concreted court-yard, stands not far from Creek Lane and the hospital outside which Mother Teresa picked up her first dying man.

The house was divided into different areas, a ward for sick children, a dormitory for well children, and a large screened area where children played and ate. By 1958, three years after opening, the home had ninety children, some of whom were left behind when their parents died in Kalighat.

Most of the children had been left as babies, in the streets, on rubbish tips, in dustbins, on doorsteps, in drains, outside police stations. Mother Teresa contacted all the local hospitals, clinics and police stations to tell them that all unwanted babies should be handed over to her.

Many babies arrived painfully small and weak because their mothers had attempted to have an abortion but failed. Sister Agnes explained: "Sometimes we get three or more babies a day. Always one for sure. More than half the number die because they are premature. I think some mothers have taken drugs to get rid of the children, which harm them; they are drugged and need a great deal of care. Still they struggle to live and some are able to survive. If they do, it is a miracle. Some weigh less than two pounds, they are unable to suck and must be fed through the nose or by injection until they are strong enough to suck."

However sick the babies are, they are wanted. Mother Teresa says, "Even if they die an hour later, let them come, the babies must not die uncared for and unloved. Because even a baby can feel. If we refuse them then we are closing our doors and these babies will be killed. It is better they die a natural death in their time than be killed."

One volunteer worker remembers: "Mother Teresa would visit Shishu Bhavan every morning. She would go from one baby to the next, and if she spotted one which was so frail and sick that it would obviously die that day, she would wrap it in a blanket and give it to one of the helpers to hold with the instruction to love that child until it died. What mattered was that no child in her care should have died without having experienced love."

As the reputation of Shishu Bhavan spread, many people began to show an interest in adopting the children, both within India and outside. Families in Sweden, Switzerland, France, Ireland, Germany, Canada and the United States applied for exit visas from the Indian authorities, which were quietly granted. Even Hindu families in India adopted children, something that had never happened before.

Mother Teresa kept a large photograph album to remind her of the many children who had gone to new homes. There were photographs of children of all sizes and ages, under cowboy hats in America, tobogganing in Switzerland, riding in England, celebrating Christmas in Germany, and driving with their new parents in France. "I'm fighting abortion with adoption," said Mother Teresa. "Abortion is nothing but fear of the child – fear to have to feed one more child, to have to educate one more child, to have to love one more child."

Most adoptions were successful but one or two failed. Douglas, an Anglo-Indian boy with a disfigured face, had been abandoned by his parents when they emigrated to England. Mother Teresa was given funds to arrange for an operation to remodel his face, which was successful, and a European family took him into their home, intending to adopt him. Sadly the parents split up and Douglas was sent back to Shishu Bhavan.

Seeing the familiar face of Mother Teresa, Douglas asked anxiously, "Mother, you want me, don't you?" "I'll always want you," she replied. A couple of years later Douglas contracted pneumonia and died, but he left this world knowing that he was a loved and wanted boy.

Six-year-old Shadona Mukherjee was picked up on the street as she lay beside her dying mother. Thin, pale-skinned with short cropped hair, no one had ever seen her smile. She cried for her brother who had been sent from Shishu Bhavan for treatment at a hospital. She ate her meals quietly and played obediently with the other children, but her expression always remained the same, fearful and sad.

When her brother, Pachu, was brought back to the home a tiny flicker of a smile began to show. One day, after a regular visitor tied a bright blue satin ribbon in her hair, she grinned. It was the first smile the Sisters had ever seen.

The children included teenage girls who were at risk when their parents died or separated. Uneducated and poor, if they were not married by the age of fifteen or sixteen there was a real danger that they would be drawn into prostitution. Some were picked up by the police and jailed, but Mother Teresa persuaded them to let her take responsibility for the girls.

Knowing they were secure and wanted, the girls enjoyed looking after the tiny babies and taking care of themselves. The Sisters taught them skills that would enable them to earn a living and be independent. Learning about hygiene, to speak English and to type, meant these girls could escape from the poverty that had haunted the lives of their families.

Mother Teresa was especially concerned about one girl, Jyoti Biswas, a strong, attractive eighteen-year-old, with long shiny black braided plaits. Mother Teresa feared Jyoti would never marry as her father had suffered with leprosy, and her mother had tuberculosis. After her father was murdered, the teenager had nursed her sick mother until her death.

Although cleared of leprosy herself, it was discovered that her two younger brothers had it. Jyoti knew that most men would avoid her because of her family and decided that she wanted to stay with the Sisters for ever, but unexpectedly an eligible man proposed to her and she married.

Mother Teresa and her Sisters were delighted and gladly provided cooking utensils, a bed, some towels and other necessities, and arranged for Jyoti and her husband to have their own home. To complete their joy, Jyoti and her husband left Shishu Bhavan and worked with leprosy sufferers who had been rejected by their families.

Over the years the Sisters watched many of their orphaned children grow up to become happily married. Sister Agnes particularly remembered a young boy, Sukomal. "One day Mother Teresa found him sitting under a tree. He'd lost his parents and was staying with his aunt and uncle who used to make him work, work, work and not give him enough to eat. So he ran away and was begging and stealing when Mother found him. So Mother brought him to Shishu Bhavan.

"He studied and went to technical school and started work, but he wanted to get married as quickly as possible. When Mother asked him why he was in such a hurry to get married he said, 'How long can I stay like this? I have nobody to call my own.' So two of us went to his village for his wedding because he had to have somebody from his family to stand in. I bought him his clothes and Mother bought him a plot of land where he built a house for his new wife."

Shishu Bhavan also became a centre for feeding the hungry, with the support of the American charity, Catholic Relief Services, who regularly sent shipments of food via Calcutta's ports. Each morning the food was cooked in enormous vats and was collected take-away style by families who queued with their own containers for the protein-rich rice or wheat.

Because local government clinics could not cope with the sheer volume of patients queuing for help, the home also provided a clinic every Saturday afternoon for local women. Many of the patients appeared to be elderly, with their deeply lined faces and leathery tough skin, but most had no idea how old they really were. "The only way we can estimate the age of the women who come to us," explained the doctor, "is by getting the approximate age of the children, and even grandchildren. We guess they are sixteen or seventeen when the first child is born. Many look old but may only be in their early forties."

Another problem that concerned Mother Teresa was that of the homeless people who slept, lived, cooked and begged on the station platforms of Sealdah Station. Hundreds of Hindu refugees poured over the border every day to escape from largely Muslim East Pakistan, and many, having nowhere to go, made their homes on the station.

By night, hundreds of figures, men, women and children, huddled together, sleeping on the cold, stone floor, covered by dirty sheets, rags or newspapers. By day, the activities of everyday life carried on as normally as possible. People washed out of brass or aluminium pots filled with water from the waiting room taps. Women cooked over tiny stoves of baked mud, using dried dung as fuel.

With food aid provided by American

Christians, Mother Teresa organized the distribution of a nourishing bulgur wheat and soy mixture. For those unable to cook for themselves, food was cooked on certain days each week, ensuring that no-one starved.

Mother Teresa estimated some ten thousand people lived in or around the station. Their sweating and fevered bodies mingled with the fumes of hundreds of stoves, the steam trains and the smells of mouldy food and decaying rubbish. Where beetles scuttled into dark corners, people sat huddled with open stretched hands, imploring passers-by to spare them a coin.

Wherever possible, the Missionaries of Charity tried to alleviate the suffering. A naked, starving child with untreated skin infections would be taken to Shishu Bhavan Home to be fed and cared for until he was strong and healthy. Clothes were given out to those whose own were threadbare and discoloured. A dying man or woman would be carried to the Home of the Dying, where they could spend their last hours knowing human love.

For Mother Teresa, caring for the dying, the unwanted children and the homeless was just the beginning. She then decided it was time to turn her attention to those most despised by society – leprosy victims.

CHAPTER FOUR

Since Bible times people who suffer from leprosy have been treated cruelly, forced to live and die with one another, kept as far away as possible from the rest of society.

Although leprosy does not kill and in its early stages is easily treatable, it basically destroys the human body little by little, making the victim helpless and ugly. The leprosy germ takes a long time to show its effects, but the first signs are white patches appearing on the skin which feel numb. Unless it is checked at this stage the nerves become so damaged that the patient may suffer paralysis, blindness and bone damage. Sufferers may cut or burn themselves without feeling any pain, which can lead to losing hands, toes and other parts of the body.

In Calcutta, hundreds of leprosy sufferers lived together in the slums, often isolated from their families and friends who feared they would be contaminated too. It was in these areas that Mother Teresa proposed to have leprosy clinics, beginning with Mohti Jihl, where her first slum school opened.

However, a local councillor objected. "What, so close to our house? That won't do!" he spluttered angrily. But his protest gave Mother Teresa an exciting idea: "We will have mobile clinics." And she told the councillor, "Bless you, Councillor, you have increased our efficiency ten times."

At about the same time, Eileen Egan, a representative of an American aid agency, the Catholic Relief Services, visited Mother Teresa to ask if she needed any help. Mother Teresa had no hesitation. "I need a mobile clinic to carry help to the poorest of our poor, the ones who cannot get to the hospital at all."

Within days the money was made available and a van was transformed into a mini medical centre. Local volunteer doctors visited four different areas of the city each week, examining people for the first signs of leprosy and treating those already infected, and a small laboratory was set up at Shishu Bhavan to identify particular problems.

The need for a mobile clinic became even more vital when Mother Teresa failed to persuade the health authorities to keep a leprosy hospital open, because people objected to having leprosy victims in their neighbourhood.

As soon as the mobile clinic arrived at the appointed time, groups of leprosy sufferers would converge on the medical team. Some arrived, hobbling slowly on deformed legs. Others whose legs could no longer support them, were carried and pulled along in makeshift wooden trolleys. Watched by curious on-lookers they would be examined and treated on the spot.

At one of their stops, Mother Teresa was introduced to Mary, whose story she found particularly sad. Mary, a poor Christian from the south of India, married a non-Christian and gave birth to their first child, a girl. Afterwards her husband married three other wives and forced Mary to beg and become a prostitute. When she discovered she had leprosy, her husband threw her out.

For those patients who received regular medication, especially once leprosy had been identified, there were clear signs of improvement. At Mohti Jihl, a sixteen-year-old orphan boy with an ugly, swollen face was treated, and within weeks was looking healthy and happy.

Dhappa was probably the area of Calcutta most heavily infected with leprosy. Along the banks of the Dhappa canal, a foul-smelling sewer, were numerous slaughter houses that provided beef and pork for Calcutta butchers to sell. Vultures congregated overhead, swooping down from time time time to feast on animal carcases.

In this neglected and forsaken corner of Calcutta lived a large number of families who were infected by leprosy. Their windowless mud huts surrounded an open space muddy with swamp water. Many who had suffered with leprosy for many years lived here, shunned by society, ashamed of their gross deformities and scarred faces. People who had once had successful careers were now reduced to living here, people like Thomas Williams, an Anglo-Indian, who had served as a steward on ocean liners until leprosy had begun to attack his hands, turning them into useless stumps.

The mobile clinic not only provided reliable medical care and attention, but was also a wonderful reminder that leprosy victims were not totally forgotten.

For some sufferers the Sisters represented the only family they had. One man told his story: "Some years ago I was a very big man and I was working in offices in a large building as a government official. I had air conditioning and people to answer me at every call. I had people bowing to me when I used to come out of my office, and I had a big family. But as soon as they discovered I had leprosy that all went. There was no more air conditioning, no fans, no home, no family – only these young Sisters who wanted me and who are my people now."

Following on from the success of the slum school in Mohti Jihl, Mother Teresa began to set up similar schools in other deprived districts of Calcutta, including Dhappa. With her American supporter, Eileen, Mother Teresa searched up and down the streets looking for a suitable site for the school.

Finding a large paved area outside a shop, Mother asked the shopkeeper if she could set up a school there and he readily agreed. A room nearby was rented from a Muslim woman to store benches, blackboards, chalk and slates, and one of the Sisters visited families who attended the leprosy clinic to announce that an open-air school would begin the next week.

On the very first day eighty-five children registered, watched from a distance by a number of suspicious parents who feared their children might be secretly taken away to hospital by the Sisters. Within a week these parents realized that the Sisters really were keeping their promises to give their children a free education.

The school, however, ran into difficulties as the noise of the traffic and of people passing on the pavement distracted the children. Another space was found underneath a jutting roof at the end of an alleyway, but again the children found it hard to concentrate. Mother Teresa decided they needed a place indoors.

Returning to the Muslim woman who had hired out a room for storage, Mother Teresa explained the need for proper classrooms. Within minutes an agreement was reached: two rooms for eight rupees a month each. Another school was born out of the determination of one woman who cared for those most people preferred to forget.

In 1956 Mother Teresa's work received a boost

when a group of influential Christian women began to campaign on behalf of leprosy sufferers. They were led by Ann Blaikie, a British woman married to a businessman based in Calcutta, who was looking for an opportunity to help others less fortunate than herself.

After contacting Mother Teresa she first organized some friends to raise funds by selling crafts, to make children's clothes and repair toys. This simple beginning led to a well-advertised Flag Day, when hundreds of volunteers stood on the streets of Calcutta to remind people of the needs of leprosy sufferers. Each one rang a bell, just as leprosy victims used to in the past, to warn people they were approaching. Posters all over the city proclaimed "Touch the Leper with Your Compassion".

The Flag Day raised plenty of money for the work, and made all kinds of people, from leprosy sufferers themselves to diplomatic officials, aware of the need to fight the prejudice which made leprosy victims outcasts of society.

Someone once thoughtlessly remarked to Mother Teresa: "I wouldn't touch or help a leper for a thousand pounds." Back came her immediate reply: "Neither would I but I would willingly tend him for the love of God."

In 1959 Ann Blaikie accompanied Mother Teresa to the opening of a permanent village where leprosy sufferers could live, at Titagarh, just outside Calcutta. Not only could they be treated here but they could also learn a skill such a weaving, shoemaking or tailoring. In this way they became self-sufficient, living on the profits made from selling their products, and did not need to rely on outside help or resort to begging.

In years to come the centre of Titagarh attracted leprosy victims from all over India. About 15,000 outpatients a year now go for diagnosis and the medicines which can prevent the disease from spreading.

In 1962, inspired by Mother Teresa's example, the Calcutta Corporation provided thirty-five acres of fertile farming land two hundred miles outside Calcutta to set up a town for leprosy victims. Known as Shantinagar, "The Place of Peace", four hundred families live and work here together, leading lives as near normal as possible.

The first arrivals learnt to make bricks and then built whitewashed homely cottages for those who were yet to come. They grew their own rice, made baskets, raised cattle and poultry, while one group set up their own printing press.

At a small hospital, in spotlessly clean wards, the Sisters cared for those with serious symptoms, and gave appropriate medical attention to less serious cases in the outpatients department. Any children born in Shantinagar were given special care and attention to ensure they were not infected by their parents.

By 1958 the Missionaries of Charity had become an acceptable feature of Calcutta's streets, and Mother Teresa's dream was to have one hundred Sisters, some of whom she wanted to send to other parts of India. Invitations had come from Bishops in many different areas, but Archbishop Perier was anxious that her Order should restrict itself to Calcutta for the first ten years of its life. However, he relaxed this rule and in 1959, not quite ten years since Mother Teresa first set out on her lonely journey into the slums, a team of Sisters left for Ranchi.

By now a Sister's life had developed into a distinctive and recognizable pattern. Along with her two saris, sandals, crucifix and bucket, each Sister had a metal spoon and plate, simple possessions identical to those of the poor they were helping. The Sisters always travelled to the slums in pairs, each carrying a plain green bag containing an old glass bottle that had once held cooking oil, filled with water.

Mother Teresa gave them clear instructions about what to do if offered food. "Our people always want to say 'Thank you' to the Sisters," Mother Teresa said, "and they offer them a cup of tea, maybe the last thing they have. Or perhaps they will buy a sweet to be ready for the Sisters for tea. Then we began to have invitations from the better-off families. The simple answer is that the Sisters cannot accept anything – from the richest to the poorest. That way nobody feels hurt."

Rising at twenty to five each morning, the Sisters left for chapel where, following the Indian custom, they removed their sandals and knelt barefoot for half an hour of prayer and meditation. Each morning they would pray: "Take, O Lord, and receive all our liberty, our memory, our understanding and our whole will, whatever we have and possess. You have given us all these; to you, O Lord, we restore them; all are yours, dispose of them in any way according to your will. Give us your love and your grace, for this is enough for us."

At six o'clock everyone attended Communion, remembering the Last Supper when Jesus offered Himself as the victim for the sin of the world. Each time they received the broken bread and the wine they were reminded of the broken lives Jesus was calling them to love.

After tea and chapattis they set out for Shishu Bhavan, Kalighat, the slum schools, the leprosy clinics or Sealdah station. Some walked, others took the tramcars. Returning to headquarters just after midday, they ate stew with rice or wheat, washed up, then lay down for a short rest. By now the Sisters had been up and about for seven hours and had done the equivalent of a full day's work.

The second part of the day was just as busy. From two to six o'clock they were out on the streets again, returning for worship in the chapel followed by supper. Then came a time for fun and laughter, rest and reading, and by ten o'clock most were ready for sleep. A few worked overnight at Shishu Bhavan, while trained helpers were entrusted with night duty at Kalighat.

The work was so varied and unpredictable there was little chance to feel bored. Every Thursday the Sisters stayed at headquarters to clean their rooms, study and catch up on chores such as mending. Thursday was also a time when they might picnic, cook sweets, sing traditional Indian songs and dance.

Their work that day was carried out by the novices, those who were training to be nuns, who spent the rest of the week studying theology, church history and the Bible. Each novice was free to leave the society at any time during her first three years of training, which culminated with her first vows of commitment. These vows were renewed in the fourth and fifth year, and lifetime vows were taken after six years.

As the work grew Mother Teresa found herself answering more and more letters. Working late into the night, she would write out each letter by hand, giving a personal reply to each one. When asked how she managed to keep up such a demanding schedule she once replied with a mischievous smile "I sleep fast".

By 1960 the work was well established with one hundred and nineteen Sisters, and Mother Teresa began to receive requests from outside India to speak about her work. She was particularly eager to meet those who had been supporting her work with money and prayer in America. For the first time since her arrival in India in 1929, she prepared to leave for an international speaking tour.

Las Vegas, famous for gambling, nightclubs and quickie divorces in nearby Reno, was her unlikely destination, where she was to speak to over three thousand Catholic women. Armed with her first Indian passport, travelling alone, Mother Teresa must have looked a curious sight in her plain sandals and cheap cotton sari.

Standing before her enormous audience in a vast horse-shoe shaped hall Mother Teresa first placed her hands together, palm to palm, in the traditional Indian manner and bowed her head. She continued, "I have never spoken in public before. This is the first time and to be here with you and to be able to tell you the love story of God's mercy for the poorest of the poor – it is a grace of God."

She then went on to describe some of the many people who were being helped by the work of the Missionaries of Charity. "We in India love our children. The mothers, as poor as they may be, cling to their children. A leper woman, living away from Titagarh, one of our centres, had heard that the Sisters were taking care of leprosy sufferers. She had it herself and she had a child of two. Bhakti was her name. Bhakti means love. She walked miles to the clinic just to make sure her little Bhakti didn't have the disease.

"She thought she saw on her body a white spot, the sign of the disease. And though her own feet were partly eaten away, and her hands were without fingers, still this brave woman, this loving woman, carried the child all the way for several miles to the Sisters to make sure that her child did not have leprosy. And when the Sisters examined her and found that the child was safe, she was so happy she was not afraid to walk back all the way. Examples such as these happen daily, and the joy and the happiness these people share – it is you who share it."

Mother Teresa went on to say she was not going to ask for further aid. "I don't beg. I have not begged from the time we started the work. But I go to the people – the Hindus, the Muslims, and the Christians – and I tell them, 'I have come to give you a chance to do something beautiful for God.' And the people, they want to do something beautiful for God and they come forward."

After the speech, Mother Teresa visited the exhibition hall where, sitting by a stand, she talked to one person after another. Although nothing was said, she was aware that people were slipping money into her plain canvas bag. It became so full it had to be emptied again and again.

Before leaving Las Vegas, Mother Teresa found one souvenir to remind her of her visit. Having been driven out to see the Nevada desert, she settled down near a cactus plant to spend time in silent meditation. Picking up a few of the long cactus spines, she wove them into a circle of thorns which she carried all the way back to Calcutta, where she placed it on the head of the crucified Christ hanging in the convent's chapel.

From Las Vegas Mother Teresa flew to the state of Illinois, to address another group of loyal supporters who were especially interested in the slum projects. Mother Teresa told them how God worked to bring about another Mother and Child clinic. "The whole convent and the children in the slums prayed, and it was very strange that the same week we got the answer. By the morning mail we heard from your group that you had vowed to help our Mother and Child clinic.

"In the afternoon I had a letter from an English lady doctor who had seen the work and wanted to help. Next day I got a letter to say that the land I had been looking for could be ours. So the place, the money and the persons to do the work came as an answer to prayer."

After the meeting Mother Teresa visited New

York and saw for herself the suffering people of American society. Taken on a tour of the slums of New York, Mother Teresa met a man slumped on the pavement, leaning against a wall with his eyes half shut. "What can we do for him?" she asked her companion, who explained that the man was drunk not dying.

The man opened his eyes and waved his hand indicating he wanted them to walk on. As they carried on past shabby boarding houses, other men in filthy jumpers and torn overcoats staggered by them, their faces anxious and strained. For Mother Teresa it was difficult to pass by any man who was clearly in need. Her friends had to explain that such people were the responsibility of the New York Police, who would take them to hospital if necessary or a state-run alcoholics centre where they might sober up.

While in New York, Mother Teresa visited the headquarters of the United Nations to talk with a representative of the World Health Organization. She was actually met by the Director, who listened intently as Mother Teresa described her work amongst leprosy patients in the Calcutta slums. Close to tears, the Director promised Mother Teresa that supplies would be made available through the Indian Government.

From the States, Mother Teresa flew to Germany via Britain, where she was briefly reunited with her friend Ann Blaikie, who had now returned to live near London. Working with a number of wives of businessmen who had returned to England from Calcutta, Ann was spreading news of Mother Teresa's projects and encouraging prayer and giving.

Having appeared briefly on British television, Mother Teresa was becoming better known, and Ann Blaikie found herself increasingly busy responding to letters from enthusiastic supporters. A Mother Teresa Committee was set up which later grew into an international support group known as The Association of Co-Workers.

In Germany, Mother Teresa was welcomed by the head of a Christian charity, who was ready to offer help with her next project, a Home for the Dying in Delhi. Although Mother Teresa explained the Home would never be able to pay for its own upkeep, the charity was willing to finance the whole cost of building a new home.

Although nearing the end of her tour, Mother Teresa still had two major appointments to prepare for, both in Rome. One was to meet her brother Lazar for the first time in over thirty years. The other was to meet the Pope, to ask if the Missionaries of Charity could come under his special care and be allowed to begin their work outside India.

CHAPTER FIVE

Towards the end of the Second World War, Mother Teresa's brother Lazar had escaped death when occupying forces had decided to shoot him. His brave Italian wife, Maria, had thrown herself across her husband's body so she would have to be shot first. For some reason their attackers changed their mind.

Now living in exile in southern Italy, Lazar had started a new life helped by the Catholic Relief Services, the same organization that supported Mother Teresa's work. He had no news of their mother, Drana, or sister, Age, who now lived in Tirana, the capital of Albania, a country which had become increasingly repressive and isolated from the rest of the world since it became a communist republic in 1945.

Travelling to Rome, Lazar, with his wife Maria and ten-year-old daughter, Agi, was reunited with his sister, and they were able to talk about happy memories. With no means of contacting Drana and Age, and no sign of their leaving Albania, they could only speculate on what might be happening.

Thankful for their time together, Mother Teresa next turned her attention to her work.

She was told her proposal for her Order would be dealt with by two high ranking deputies, but she had permission to attend a special Communion held by Pope John XXIII in the Sistine Chapel. Stepping forward to kiss his ring, Mother Teresa met his gentle gaze and he quietly asked God to continue protecting her.

After examining in great detail all the principles on which the Missionaries of Charity were founded, the Pope's deputies asked Mother Teresa many questions about her Order. They were particularly intrigued by her ability to help the poorest of the poor without regular financial backing. Confidently, Mother Teresa explained that they depended solely on God who had never disappointed them, and emphasized that the Sisters chose to live very simply themselves.

Having given her own account of the work Mother Teresa was free to return to India, where she decided to concentrate on expanding the work within India while waiting for the final outcome.

With work established in Ranchi and Patna, teams of Sisters moved further afield to other Indian states, Uttar Pradesh in the north, the Punjab in the far north-west, Maharashtra in the west, and Madhya Pradesh in central India. The Sisters, accustomed to conditions in Calcutta, were well able to cope with their new responsibilities and adapt to different environments.

In 1962 an unexpected honour enabled Mother

Teresa to build another children's home, when a Sister phoned Mother from Agra to say there was a desperate need for a home which would cost 50,000 rupees. Mother Teresa did not have the money. "I told her it was impossible. Then the telephone rang again. This time it was from a newspaper, saying I'd been given the Magsaysay Award from the Philippines. I asked, 'How much is it?' The man replied, 'About 50,000 rupees, Mother.' So I called the Sister back to tell her God must want a children's home in Agra."

Two years later Mother Teresa sent another four teams from Calcutta to Darjeeling, close to the convent where she first trained to be a nun, to Goa on the west coast, to Trivandrum in the far north, and to Jamshedpur in the neighbouring state of Bihar. Many joys and some disappointments were reported, but one tragedy in particular highlighted the risks and sacrifices the Sisters were taking to help others.

Sister Leonia, a qualified doctor, was in charge of their work in Madhya Pradesh. Returning to Calcutta for a meeting, she developed alarming symptoms. When she started to brush her teeth, she began to make dry, barking sounds and her body went into spasms. At the hospital they diagnosed rabies.

Months before she had rescued a puppy from a pack of dogs and been bitten. The doctor informed Mother Teresa, "She will be dead within forty-eight hours." Sitting by her bedside, holding her hand, Mother Teresa told Sister Leonia, "I have received you into this work for Jesus. I will be with you to help you go from us to Him." Within two days Sister Leonia was dead.

Also in 1964 the Archbishop of Melbourne, James Knox, organized the visit of Pope Paul VI to Bombay for a major conference, and at the end of his visit the Pope presented Mother Teresa with his white ceremonial motor car, informally nick-named the "Pope-mobile".

The car, a 1964 Ford Lincoln, had been especially designed and manufactured for the event and was a gift to the Pope from an American University. Although it had only been used for a few hours the Pope offered it to Mother Teresa "To share in her universal mission of love".

Mother Teresa clearly had no intention of driving around in a luxurious limousine herself, and there were suggestions that it could be converted into an ambulance or hearse. But Mother Teresa had an even better idea. With permission from the government, Mother Teresa arranged to raffle the Pope-mobile and raised almost £37,500, five times what the car was worth at the time. The car was won by a young Indian accountant studying at the time in Britain, who resold it, sending a large amount of the proceeds to Mother Teresa. With the money from the raffle Mother Teresa built a new hospital at Shantinagar, the settlement for leprosy sufferers.

The Order continued to grow, numbering over three hundred Sisters by 1965. Behind the scenes, Archbishop James Knox was making efforts to ensure the Missionaries of Charity had papal authority to increase their work. On 1st February of that year they received official confirmation that the Missionaries of Charity were the responsibility of the Pope himself and were now free to expand wherever God would lead.

The first invitation to help came from Venezuela, South America, where Bishop Benitez was concerned about the plight of poor uneducated women who lived in fertile, rural areas where they were at risk of being exploited by wealthy landowners and developers.

Mother Teresa wanted to see the situation for herself rather than send her Sisters out into the unknown. Escorted by Spanish missionary priests, Father Tomas and Father Manuel, Mother Teresa was driven into a remote jungle area called "Zone Negra" (Black Belt). Travelling over rough dirt tracks through fields of sugar cane and groves of pale green limes, the priests described the problems to Mother Teresa.

They told her that the people who lived there could live fairly comfortably growing their own produce. However, rich outsiders were offering large sums of money to buy the fields. Once the money was spent, the people had to search for a job so that they could buy food they used to grow for themselves.

In a small town, Cocorote, the priests showed Mother Teresa the local church, which they visited from time to time as there was no priest living there. Next door to the church was an empty building that could house a priest had there been one. "Our Sisters will come here," said Mother Teresa, knowing that Father Tomas and Father Manuel would take good care of them.

Within a year of her visit, Mother Teresa sent a team of four Indian Sisters to set up base in Cocorote but first they had to seek permission from the Indian Government to work overseas. For many years India had been on the receiving end of missionaries from all over the world, so it was an historic moment when the Sisters applied for passports and visas.

When the Sisters arrived at Cocorote, in July 1965, they found the local people had been busy preparing the home for them, providing comfortable armchairs, a large sofa, attractive curtaining and a refrigerator. Wanting to keep their lifestyle as simple as possible, the Sisters gave these things away to poor families and replaced them with plainer versions. The curtains were imaginatively recycled by the poor into bedcovers and dresses.

Using donated sewing machines, cloth and typewriters, the Sisters began with sewing and typing classes for local girls, some of whom asked for English lessons, which were also started. Discovering that squatters, two families who had migrated from the mountain areas, lived in a neighbouring building, the Sisters took them soap and clean clothes and began visiting them regularly. They were the only visitors the new-comers ever had.

Grateful for the work the Sisters were doing, the local community helped in all kinds of ways. They gave the Sisters an estate car and helped them to drive it over the unmade roads so that they could reach people who lived in the surrounding villages. A butcher began sending meat, and each morning a street trader con-tributed a few tortillas, thin pancakes, which reminded the Sisters of their Indian chappatis.

Because of their dark skins, the Sisters were easily accepted by the local people who called them "our Sisters". The Sisters were welcomed into the poorest of homes, often by people who wanted someone to listen to their problems. After visiting the home of Mrs Rumbo regularly, she allowed them to meet her fourth child, Rosameli, who suffered from polio. She had been hiding the child from them, ashamed of her handicap and her lack of clothes. Unable to walk, six-year-old Rosameli crawled around on hands and knees, a habit which was making her back curve inwards. The Sisters readily offered to bring new clothes and to find out about therapy.

Although they were poor, many of the women the Sisters were helping had a large number of children, often to different partners. Fearful of growing old and helpless, unable to earn a living and look after themselves, the women hoped these children would grow up and provide for them in their old age.

When the Sisters realized that many of the women had a low opinion of themselves and lacked the confidence to change their lives, the Sisters decided to concentrate on teaching the women skills. Once the women found they had abilities which could earn them money, they began to understand that they would make choices about the kind of life they led.

The work had been progressing for almost a year when Mother Teresa decided to visit the Sisters in Cocorote. On this trip Mother Teresa learnt that the Sisters had been offered a block of ruins that had once been a hotel, and went along to inspect it. The site had become a rubbish tip, populated with rats and snakes, and was overrun with bushes and green ivy. But Mother Teresa could see the potential. "The space is good", she said. "Let us get the people to help us clean it up and then we can see what we can do with it."

The local people cleared away the rubbish and in a few years there was a training centre that also served as a hostel for the homeless.

On her way back to Calcutta, Mother Teresa stopped off in Rome to make a personal plea to the Albanian Embassy, in the hope that her mother and sister in Albania could be allowed to migrate to Italy. Her brother Lazar could give them a home but he could not go to the Embassy himself as the Albanians had blacklisted him.

Their mother, Drana, and sister, Age, had both moved away from Skopje and were now living in the capital city of Albania, Tirana, from where they were able to send letters from time to time. Although Lazar had tried through French diplomats to persuade the authorities to let Drana and Age leave the country, the only response they received was a statement saying "Mrs Drana Bojaxhiu and Miss Age Bojaxhiu are not physically fit to travel abroad."

Lazar was not convinced. "My mother and sister were not ill or confined to bed. Their only illness was that of solitude and hopelessness."

In the company of her American supporter, Eileen Egan, Mother Teresa stood on the steps of the Albanian Embassy and rang the bell. After her third attempt a man opened the door. He looked puzzled as if he was unused to having visitors. "Sou de Schipteru" (I am from Albania) said Mother Teresa .

Ushered into a dark, shuttered room, the man turned on the electric lights instead of opening the shutters to let in the morning sunshine. The furniture was shrouded in white sheets and the floor was bare wood. After sitting down Mother Teresa repeated her introductory words "Sou de

Schipteru". The man burst into a flood of Albanian words.

Turning to her American friend, Mother Teresa said, "I can't find the words in my mother tongue. It's too far back."

On her behalf Eileen Egan explained in Italian that Mother Teresa was from an Albanian family and that she had not seen her family in the last forty years as she had gone to India to become a nun. She described how Mother Teresa had decided to serve the poor and how many young women had joined her.

"Her group is called the Missionaries of Charity", Eileen continued. "While her name is Agnes Gonxha Bojaxhiu, she is known to everyone as Mother Teresa. Although she has become an Indian citizen everyone knows where she comes from and she has brought great honour to Albania."

Mother Teresa then asked him if he spoke Serbo-Croatian and as he did she told him more. He listened intently, brushing away a few tears at one point in the conversation, and asked for more details of her work in Calcutta. Eileen related the work of the Home for the Dying and the slum schools.

"You say, signora, that this small woman has started all this work?" he replied, looking incredulously at the sari-clad woman with bare feet in flat sandals.

"I consider that she is one of the best-known

Albanians outside of your country", Eileen added.

"I will do my best for her. I will explain to the attaché. You must come back tomorrow at the same hour."

As they walked away from the Embassy, Eileen asked Mother Teresa what she had said to the man that had brought him close to tears.

"I only told him the truth, that I came as a child seeking for its mother. Then I explained that my mother is old and ill. She is eighty-one and longs to see me, as I long to see her after so many years. I told him that I was helpless to do anything and that only the Albanians could give her permission to come to Rome."

The next day the attaché was waiting for them. He spoke some words in Albanian to Mother Teresa, promising to make contact with the government in Tirana.

In the meantime Eileen and Mother Teresa made arrangements for Drana and Age to have a temporary home in Rome, and they sent a message instructing them, if they received exit visas, to come to Rome where they would be met.

When Mother Teresa and Eileen next went to the Embassy another staff member talked to them. "The attaché has left Rome. I have no news about the exit visas."

Eileen said afterwards, "When Mother Teresa left the Embassy, for the first time I saw tears in her eyes. She looked up and said, 'O God, I understand and accept my own sufferings. But it is hard to understand and accept my mother's, when all she desires in her old age is to see us again'."

The day after their last visit to the Embassy in Rome, Drana wrote to Mother Teresa , "Even if we never meet again in this sad world, we shall surely meet in heaven."

After numerous calls to the Embassy no exit visas were ever granted. Mother Teresa appealed to influential people to help but they too were unsuccessful. She admitted to her brother, "Up to now I have managed to obtain everything through love and prayer . . . but there are still walls and obstacles that even love cannot knock down."

Two years later Drana died. Age wrote, "I have been very depressed since I was left without our poor mother. How I miss her! But she has left us and will not return . . . I hope I can get permission to come to you, and then everything will be easier." But her wish was never granted and she died in Albania without seeing her brother or sister again.

Although Mother Teresa could bring hope and help to the most miserable situations she was helpless to do anything about her own family's suffering.

In Calcutta, Mother Teresa grieved their loss, and with God's help renewed her efforts to help those she could. With the work of the Sisters well established in Venezuela the next request for help came surprisingly from the Pope himself, who asked Mother Teresa to start a new work in Rome.

With a cheque for ten thousand dollars from the Pope, Mother Teresa said, "I am prepared to open a House if there really are poor people here."

She went to the city outskirts and discovered away from the tourist spots and sophisticated town houses, acres of shantytowns. Makeshift homes sprawled for miles, offering basic shelter and protection for immigrant families from the poorer south. Orange-red terracotta tiles formed the flat roofs, which were often weighted down by heavy stones. Many of the occupants had planted small gardens and vines, some had illegally tapped into the city's electricity supplies.

Returning to the Pope she said, "Your Holiness, God has given us plenty of work." Soon a team of ten Sisters had moved into a large bare building in the heart of one shantytown, Tor Fiscale, and transformed the empty shell into a dormitory, chapel, kitchen and washroom. Once they were organized the Sisters began to visit local homes, and discovered many elderly people living alone in ramshackle huts.

One old gentleman of ninety-three was barely able to leave his bed. Critical and suspicious of people who believed in God, he could not resist asking why the Sisters cared for him so cheerfully without asking to be paid. When the Sister told him about Jesus and His teaching to love one another, the old man was deeply moved.

One day the man said to the Sister, "You have brought me God. Now bring me the priest."

The priest listened as the old man asked God to forgive him his sins. He died not long after. It was a story that Mother Teresa often related.

In 1970, two years after the Sisters arrived in Rome, a group of English students spent their summer holidays enlarging the convent and building a large community centre alongside. The young people living in Tor Fiscale also joined in and made friends with the students. They admitted it wasn't until they saw the Sisters at work that they realized they needed to do something about poverty in their own community.

One story illustrates that not everyone in the area understood the work. One day a group of students knocked at the door of a local priest asking if he could direct them to Mother Teresa. He replied, "If you mean those Indian nuns who go round looking for gypsies and living with them, yes, I can tell you where they are. They are a disgrace to the Church."

The centre was put to various uses, acting as a day-care crèche for mothers, many of whom were single parents who earned whatever they could by doing domestic work. Young girls and women came to a sewing class, learning to sew by hand and machine. At five o'clock each evening the centre was filled with youngsters, completing their homework in peace and quiet because their homes were too noisy and crowded. If they needed any help the Sisters were on hand to answer questions and check their work.

If Rome seemed a surprising venue for the Missionaries of Charity then how much more surprising that their next invitation came from Melbourne, Australia, where Archbishop James Knox was already an enthusiastic supporter of Mother Teresa. Out of deep concern for the plight of Aborigines, he asked Mother Teresa to send Sisters to Bourke, New South Wales, and having seen the situation for herself, she readily agreed.

Bourke is deep in the Australian outback, surrounded by thousands of miles of desert. Although the first inhabitants of Australia, the Aboriginal community were treated as outcasts by most of Australian society, as were certain groups of people in India. Wisely, to begin the work there Mother Teresa selected Indian Sisters who would understand what it felt like to be discriminated against.

The Sisters shared their convent with the Aborigines, organizing sewing classes and cookery lessons for the women and a library and art activities for school children. They took a special interest in the children, as from an early age many became heavy drinkers and played truant from school.

Many of the Aborigines found it difficult to make the adjustment from being farmers who worked for themselves, to being paid workmen who were expected by their white employers to keep to strict timetables. Some of them lost their jobs because they were tempted to wander off or go "walkabout" instead of working. The Sisters tried to befriend many of these men, helping them to feel accepted and loved.

When Mother Teresa paid the Sisters a visit she made friends with an old man who lived alone. He sat in the dark while a beautiful lamp stayed unused, covered in dust. After cleaning out his room, Mother Teresa asked why he did not light the lamp.

"There's no one to light it for", he replied.

"If the Sisters come to visit you, will you light it?" she asked.

"Yes," he answered, "I will light it if I hear the sound of a human voice."

The promise of human company brought a sense of worth and dignity to a man who thought he was of no value to anyone.

Slowly but surely the work of the Missionaries of Charity was spreading into all corners of the world, bringing light to those in darkness and hope to the helpless.

CHAPTER SIX

The work of the Missionaries of Charity began to gain worldwide attention when a gifted British journalist, author and broadcaster, Malcolm Muggeridge, found himself captivated by the person of Mother Teresa.

In 1969 a BBC television interview was arranged between Muggeridge and Mother Teresa. Muggeridge had interviewed hundreds of people before but he was overwhelmed by people's reactions to the programme when it was broadcast.

Writing later he admitted: "I cannot pretend that, after it was over, I had a feeling that something particularly memorable had been recorded in my tele-conversation with Mother Teresa . . . Technically it was barely usable, and there was some doubt as to whether it was good enough for showing at all except late at night. In the end . . . it was put out on a Sunday evening. The response was greater than I have known to any comparable programme, both in mail and in contributions of money for Mother Teresa's work . . . They came from young and old, rich and poor, educated and uneducated; all sorts and conditions of people. All of them said approximately the same thing – this woman spoke to me as no one ever has, and I feel I must help her.''

By popular demand the programme was repeated quite soon after its first showing, and again resulted in a flood of letters and donations. Altogether some £20,000 was received even though no appeal for money had been made. After this experience Muggeridge had a passionate desire to go to Calcutta and make a television programme about her and her work.

In 1969, having persuaded the BBC to finance the project, Muggeridge and his team arrived in Calcutta for five days' filming. Although Mother Teresa was deeply suspicious of the filming process she agreed, on condition that they filmed her workers going about their normal duties.

Muggeridge and his camera crew were amazed that the filming progressed with few problems. Normally a fifty-minute documentary takes two to three months but they were able to produce enough footage in the five days. Much to Muggeridge's surprise there were no breakdowns and crises, and no bickering or quarrelling.

Even more staggering was the quality of film produced when they filmed in the dim wards of Kalighat. The producer and director insisted that filming inside was impossible, but the cameraman tried nevertheless. The result showed a room bathed in an exquisite soft light which no one could explain. Although at the time Muggeridge had no faith in God he was convinced they had managed miraculously to capture the visible love of God.

The documentary was entitled "Something Beautiful for God", a favourite expression Mother Teresa used to describe her life-saving work. Muggeridge wrote a book of the same name in which he discussed the problem of suffering and admitted his own lack of faith. Twelve years later, in 1982, at the age of seventy-nine, having kept in touch with Mother Teresa over the years, he became a Christian. He wrote, "Words cannot convey how beholden I am to her."

The film and book were distributed all over the world, and for the first time in history a nun was a media personality. The book was translated into numerous languages and was also printed in Braille. Muggeridge generously insisted the royalties should be given to the work rather than to himself.

So much interest was generated by the book and film that Mother Teresa received many more invitations to be interviewed, and was mobbed by photographers and reporters at meetings and airports. Although Mother Teresa found the publicity tiring and demanding she endured the attention, convinced that the poor would ultimately benefit and that she should use every opportunity to tell others about the love of God.

An interviewer once asked Mother Teresa

what was her share in suffering for Jesus. Looking around at the battery of newspaper journalists and photographers she smiled and answered simply, "This".

It would be impossible to calculate how many people were inspired to become involved in the work as a result of seeing the film or reading the book, but at a time when fewer people were joining religious orders, the Missionaries of Charity were inundated with applicants.

By September 1970 the monsoon rains were over in Calcutta, so when a light but steady rain began to fall everyone expected it would soon stop. But the showers became heavier and heavier and beat down for over a week. The streets filled up with water, bringing the traffic to a standstill, and hundreds of fragile slum dwellings came close to collapse.

Unending queues of people trailed through the flooded streets to wait outside Shishu Bhavan in the hope of being given their one cooked meal of the day. Accustomed to catering for fewer numbers, the Sisters found there wasn't enough food to feed everyone and wondered what they were going to do.

As the floods had completely disrupted travel that day, all schools had been closed. However this left CARE, a charity that provided fresh bread to the schools in Calcutta, with vast quantities of surplus food. Aware that Mother Teresa would make good use of the food, CARE offered her the food entirely free!

Enriched with vitamins and protein, the bread was handed out to all newcomers. "It's a first-class miracle", said Mother Teresa in amazement. Among the new people who came for food was a Bengali man who insisted on seeing Mother Teresa personally. He told his story to the Sisters. "My name is Sarkar. My village is underwater and the people are sitting on the roof of the school. One baby has just been born in the next village which is also flooded. Two other mothers are ready to give birth. No one has come to help us. Mother helped us before. I must see her."

As he was speaking Mother Teresa appeared and immediately recognized him. As they spoke together, a smile came to his sad face. For the benefit of an American guest, Mother Teresa interpreted their talk. "This is Deben Sarkar, the teacher. He has been a leader of his people, all refugees from East Pakistan. The hardest workers I know. And now they are rained out. Two whole villages. We must go to them. We must be in time to save those young mothers."

With a lorry load of CARE-donated bread and the mobile clinic, a small group led by Mother Teresa and Sister Agnes drove through the rain-sodden streets towards the flooded area. Stopping in front of a large grey building, Sarkar informed them that many people were sheltering inside. The building was surrounded by a gruesome murky river of floodwater, with a few bloated dead animals floating in it.

Taking off her sandals, Mother Teresa began to wade knee-deep through the slimy waters to reach the door. Inside, she found clusters of people squashed up on benches in gloomy rooms lit only by paraffin lamps and a few candles. Once it was established how many people were taking refuge there, men waded out to the lorry and carried back hundreds of loaves on their heads. Vitamins were also distributed to mothers with babies.

Intent on rescuing Sarkar's community, the women returned to the lorry, driving further out until Sarkar spotted in the distance a group of people huddled on a roof, completely surrounded by water. As they watched a large boat came into sight and drew up to the building.

Suddenly heavy drops of rain began to fall. Mother Teresa suggested they prayed. Eventually the boats, crammed with damp and weary passengers, manoeuvred round and brought them to the soggy but relatively firm land.

"We must take all the women and children to Shishu Bhavan", said Mother Teresa. "Then I will find a place for everyone else and I will come back and pick you up." Sister Agnes stayed behind with about fifty villagers, who stood solemnly in the rain munching chunks of bread.

When the lorry returned, Mother Teresa brought the good news that accommodation had been found in a High School close to Shishu Bhavan. By the end of the day, three hundred stranded flood victims were enjoying the safety and security of a dry shelter.

The following day the Sisters handed out clothing, and Mother Teresa began planning the next step. "We will need tarpaulins and heavy poles. Then the men can start repairing the school and the houses. We'll find the food for the time being. We've got to give them work until they can go back to making mats. We can help them to sew things that can be sold."

Some time later, when the waters had receded, the villagers returned to their homes, and Mother Teresa arranged for a clinic to be opened to serve their community and others nearby.

Confident that the Sisters could cope with an emergency should it happen again, Mother Teresa prepared for another international tour, which included a visit to London where she planned to open a Missionaries of Charity house.

The ideal place was found in Southall, a working-class district, but the asking price was £9,000 and Mother Teresa insisted that she could not pay more than £6,000. However, the estate agent later phoned to say the owner was prepared to sell for £6,000 because she wanted the house to be filled with love. Only two weeks after arriving in the country, a group of Sisters led by Sister Frederick prepared to move in.

Mother Teresa herself headed up a group of

willing volunteers who scrubbed the house from top to bottom. After a few minor building alterations, a service was held by Cardinal Heenan to commemorate the opening. As it happened, the electricity workers were on strike that day and the service had to be held by flickering candlelight. Although the city of London was blacked out, Mother Teresa and her Sisters shone a light that never dimmed.

Mother Teresa had no illusions about developed, sophisticated capital cities like London. She was aware of the lonely immigrant families living in overcrowded, dilapidated rooms, of the elderly found dying alone in a comfortable home. Sister Frederick kept her informed about the many homeless men and women sleeping outside in all weathers.

In London a group of Catholics, the St Mungo Society, took Mother Teresa and Sister Frederick onto the streets where they searched out the needy, providing hot food and drink. On a cold night, her escorts knew exactly where to take their supplies. To keep warm, the homeless found spots in alleyways or on pavements where the heating systems of hotels and other large buildings filtered out through vents.

Talking to the men, Mother Teresa discovered that they were mainly poor young men from Glasgow or Dublin or country areas, who had come to London in the hope of finding work. Largely unskilled, they found jobs in hotels and restaurants cleaning or washing dishes. As their wages were low, few could afford London prices for accommodation so they ended up on the streets.

In future interviews when Mother Teresa was asked why she was working in affluent countries like England she explained, "In England, they suffer from loneliness. They have no need of bread, but they need human love. That is the hungry Christ for us . . . I have come more and more to realize that it is being unwanted that is the worst disease that any human being can ever experience. Nowadays we have found medicine for leprosy . . . there's medicine for TB . . . for all kinds of diseases there are medicines and cures. But for being unwanted, unless there are willing hands to serve and there's a loving heart to love, I don't think this terrible disease can ever be cured."

By 1970 the Missionaries of Charity were making an impact throughout the world. In all there were 585 Sisters, young women from all corners of the earth, Pakistan, Sri Lanka, Nepal, Malaysia, Germany, France, Ireland, Venezuela, Malta and Mauritania. Sisters also came from all over India including Bihar, Orissa, Madras, Goa, Punjab and Kerala.

Growing alongside the Missionaries of Charity was the dedicated group of supporters led by Ann Blaikie. In 1970 the group had been officially recognized by the Pope as "The International

Association of the Co-Workers of Mother Teresa".

The principles on which the Association was founded enabled people from all walks of life to be involved. The first principle stated "The International Association of Co-Workers of Mother Teresa consists of men, women, young people and children of all religions and denominations throughout the world, who seek to love God in their fellowmen, through wholehearted service to the poorest of the poor of all castes and creeds, and who wish to unite themselves in a spirit of prayer and sacrifice with the work of Mother Teresa and the Missionaries of Charity."

With the simplest of equipment the Association mailed thousands of newsletters to groups of Co-Workers around the world and to every Missionaries of Charity house. There were no membership fees, and any meetings were to be held without food being served so that they could be held in the homes of the poor.

A sponsorship scheme was set up whereby people promised to pay for the upkeep of an orphaned or abandoned child. People were encouraged to send medicine, equipment, clothes and hand-knitted blankets to various collection points around the country, where they were forwarded to Calcutta for use in the clinics, children's homes and centres for the sick or dying.

Expenses were kept to a minimum. The Co-Workers had no offices and no one was paid for their help. Professional people such as doctors and dentists gave their services free of charge. Borrowed garages, empty cellars, church halls and spare rooms acted as collection centres, avoiding the need to pay expensive rents.

Having seen how lack of love in the home breeds all kinds of social problems, Mother Teresa urged all Co-Workers to love their families and not to neglect those nearest to them. To Mother Teresa family life must take priority even over Co-Worker activities.

Each member was encouraged to pray daily and to live as simply as they could. Wherever possible the spiritual dimension of their work was to be emphasized; so, for example, when young people organized a sponsored walk, they were encouraged to choose a sacred place as their destination, turning the walk into a pilgrimage.

There was also a special role for those who were handicapped or chronically ill and unable to join in activities. Known as Sick and Suffering Co-Workers they were to be linked to individual members of the Missionaries of Charity.

No matter how handicapped the person, they had a crucial part to play through their suffering and prayers. Mother Teresa wrote to one member, "In reality you can do much more on your bed of pain than I running on my feet, but you and I together can do all things in Him who strengthens me."

Acting as link for the suffering Co-Workers

was Jacqueline de Decker, herself a missionary nurse in India, who had been forced to give up her work because of a paralysing illness. She had first met Mother Teresa at the hospital in Patna when Mother Teresa was learning nursing skills. Like Mother Teresa , Jacqueline, a European, wore a sari, had few possessions and worked and lived among the poor for no reward.

When it was clear that Jacqueline would have to abandon her work and return to her native Belgium, Mother Teresa wrote to her. "Why not become spiritually bound to our Society which you love so dearly? While we work in the slums, you share in the merit, the prayers, and the work with your sufferings and prayers. The work is tremendous and I need workers, it is true, but I need souls like yours to pray and suffer for the work."

Jacqueline agreed to her suggestion and began searching for other handicapped people who could be linked to a Missionary of Charity. Despite frequent pain and mobility problems, Jacqueline travelled to various countries promoting the scheme. She also spent many hours writing letters by hand to hundreds of members who included the elderly, victims of cerebral palsy and multiple sclerosis, the mentally ill, the housebound and the blind.

In time there were over five thousand members from nearly seventy countries of the world who promised to pray faithfully. Once, when writing to Sick and Suffering Co-Workers, Mother Teresa admitted: "How happy I am to have you all. Often when the work is hard, I think of you – and tell God: 'Look at my suffering children, and for their love, bless this work.' And it works immediately. So you see, you are our treasure house – the powerhouse of the Missionaries of Charity."

In 1971 a group of five Sisters, with their meagre possessions, arrived, at Kennedy Airport, New York, to set up a new home in the Bronx, a notorious area where violence, drug peddling and crime were rife. The Sisters agreed to concentrate their efforts on the needs of the young people, many of whom were from broken or unloving homes.

During the hot, steamy summer holidays the Sisters organized day camps so that young people, who would normally play on the streets, could get involved in many different activities such as woodwork, music, drama and pottery. Each day began with singing and prayer, and visits were arranged to the countryside and places of interest, such as the United Nations headquarters.

The Sisters were anxious to cater not just for physical needs but also for spiritual. One Sister explained, "New York and other cities spend enormous amounts of money for thousands of inner-city kids. Mobile swimming pools, films, puppet shows on the streets, free tickets to the zoo

and museums, as well as the daily lunch, with a carton of milk and fruit juice, and sandwiches. But
this is the difficulty, everything for the body, nothing much for the mind and soul."

The Sisters also worked in the 41st Precinct, known as Fort Apache because it resembled a besieged fortress. Gunfights and armed robberies made older residents fearful of leaving their homes, so the Sisters visited them regularly. People living in anonymous apartment blocks were especially lonely.

Mother Teresa often related the story told her by one of the Sisters. "They came to a room from which a foul stench was coming. When the room was broken into, they found a woman who had been dead four or five days. No one had come to see her. They did not even know her name. Many of the people are known only by the name of their rooms or apartments."

Like New York, Belfast, Ireland was characterized by a breakdown in law and order. In 1972 Mother Teresa took four Sisters to Belfast, equipped with two blankets each and a violin. They moved into the Catholic "ghetto" of Ballymurphy, to a council house which had previously been occupied by a Catholic priest who had been murdered as he tended a dying man. The house had been completely ransacked by vandals, so the Sisters had to clear away the debris before they could begin their work.

As a sign of unity in a divided city, the Sisters worked with a group of Anglican nuns to try to bring understanding, love and forgiveness to the local people. However, their efforts to bring harmony and peace were frustrated, as after a couple of years the Sisters were asked to leave. This was one of the few occasions when the work of the Missionaries of Charity was cut short. Undeterred the Sisters set up another house, this time in impoverished Ethiopia, North Africa.

Belfast apart, the work of the Missionaries of Charity was expanding at a phenomenal rate. One area in particular deserves special mention, that of the Missionary Brothers of Charity who were not as well known as the Sisters but were making a powerful and quiet impact in places more suited to men.

CHAPTER SEVEN

By 1963 thirteen men had expressed their desire to work among the poor in the service of Mother Teresa. Only one of the men was ordained, as most priests were reluctant to join Mother Teresa because the Catholic Church does not allow a woman to be the head of a male congregation. Living on the first floor of Shishu Bhavan, the men studied together and worked with the Sisters in the slums. They dressed simply in open-necked shirts and lightweight trousers, with only a cross pinned to their shirt to distinguished them from those they cared for.

Although not recognized as a religious Order by the Pope, Archbishop Albert D'Souza of Calcutta gave his blessing to the men on 25th March of that year. The very same day, in the neighbouring state of Bihar, a Jesuit priest, Australian Ian Travers-Ball, was being ordained. Father Travers-Ball had always been interested in working for the poor, and during the third year of his priesthood training he was sent for a month to work with the Brothers in Shishu Bhavan.

Father Travers-Ball, tall, slim and bearded, was deeply moved by the work of the men and the Sisters. Their poverty and commitment impressed him and he marvelled at their enthusiasm to go on growing spiritually even though they had no spiritual teacher.

At the end of the month Mother Teresa asked him to become the director of the male branch of the Missionaries of Charity and he agreed, on condition that his superiors gave their support.

His superiors gave him three choices. One, to remain a Jesuit and continue his teaching ministry. Two, to keep his links with the Jesuits and help establish the Missionary Brothers with Mother Teresa. Three, to leave the Jesuit Order and take over the leadership of the Brothers. He chose the third. Jokingly he used to tell people that Mother Teresa kidnapped him from the Jesuits.

Like Mother Teresa years before, he left his first call and took up a second. He was thirty-eight years old, exactly the same age as Mother Teresa had been when she changed her life's direction. Similarly, his name and title changed. He took the name Brother Andrew and was known as the General Servant.

Mother Teresa had the highest regard for him. "I think for a long time he was working to give himself totally to the poor. He is a very holy person, really very holy. He was a very gifted Jesuit in every possible way, spiritually, mentally, physically. And both of us have the same mind. That is the most extraordinary thing.

But we are so different. Naturally he is much more gifted than I, very gifted."

Ian Travers-Ball came from a comfortable middle-class family in Hawthorn, a suburb of Melbourne, Australia. Despite the disapproval of his father, he left the insurance profession and decided to train as a Jesuit priest in India.

Having appointed a leader, Mother Teresa bought a simple house in Kidderpore, Calcutta, which became the headquarters of the Brothers. As far as possible it was agreed the Brothers would not go to areas where the Sisters were already working, and they began their work by rescuing young boys who lived alone on Sealdah Station.

The work spread to another dismal station, called Howrah, on the other side of the city, across the Hooghly River. One young volunteer worker described their work: "They go regularly to the railway stations in order to show the children that someone cares for them, they chat to them and make friends with them. One of the things they do is to take a bar of soap and make sure the boys wash themselves under the water towers which are used for filling up the engines, for India still uses steam trains.

"The little boys – they may be any age from eight to fifteen – live on the stations and make money wherever possible, by carrying suitcases for the passengers on the trains. Some of the boys are refugees from Bangladesh and some are homeless. They live in gangs where the eldest boy is generally the leader and looks after the young ones. The Brothers are always cheerful and always smiling."

In Howrah the Brothers also set up a home for the dying called "Nabo Jivan" ("New Life") which began with twenty-five men. One of the men they helped spoke for all the men when he said, "We thank God for the Brothers, who became our sons in our old age to help us – as we had no one on this earth."

The aims of the Society were almost identical to those of the Sisters, the first one stating: "The general aim of the Society comes from the lips of Christ our Lord Himself: Love one another; as I have loved you so you are to love one another. If there is love among you then all will know that you are My disciples."

Following on from this, the document declared: "The special aim of the Society is to live this life of love by dedicating oneself to the service of the poor in slums on the streets, homeless boys, young men in the slums, the unemployed. Those uprooted by war and disaster will always be the special object of the Brothers' concern."

When the Brothers began to work outside India, they opened houses in many areas where the Sisters were not working, including war zones. The horror of war compelled Mother Teresa to visit Vietnam and Cambodia in 1973, but after seeing the carnage and devastation she decided against sending young women there. As they clearly needed help Brother Andrew visited Saigon, the capital of South Vietnam, to see if the Brothers could offer assistance.

Communist North Vietnam's war with the South was causing widespread poverty and suffering. Thousands of Vietnamese had fled their homes for fear of persecution, murder or torture. With eleven houses well established in India, Brother Andrew felt the time was right to spread into east Asia, and sent for a team of Indian Brothers to help set up a House of Hospitality for the homeless, widows and their children and the handicapped in Saigon.

The House grew rapidly, sheltered over sixty people, and soon a family atmosphere developed. This was largely due to the single efforts of a young mother called My Lee. She had been reduced to working as a prostitute after her husband had been killed by a stolen jeep driven by a drunk, and arrived at the home with her three small children.

Brother Andrew explained: "We took her in. She was thirty-four years of age and each of her children had a different father. She was determined to raise her children and was a careful and devoted mother. My Lee became the heart of our House of Hospitality . . . she helped make it a real community."

In the midst of great upheaval and insecurity people found peace and hope. An American

Brother wrote about the discomforts but also the privilege of being in Saigon. "Let me describe our house here in Saigon. The first floor sleeps about thirty or so shelterless people. The second floor is the same but has room for classes during the day. The third floor is for the Brothers. It consists of two small rooms in which we eat, sleep, read and pray. Each Brother has a sleeping pallet like the ones the people use and this is rolled up during the day. There is no privacy and always much noise. We feed over a hundred people a day in the house . . . The hardest thing to accept is the rats. The rain has driven them indoors and we can hear and feel them running around the floor at night.

"The people . . . are all so good to us. The children are all so well behaved and share all they have with us . . . I came to Asia to confusion and find peace. I expected to find a war, and hate, and instead I find love. Instead of despair the people have so much joy. And we share in their joy. It is good to be here."

In addition to the House of Hospitality the Brothers opened up houses for the physically and mentally handicapped who had no one to care for them. However, only two years after arriving the Brothers were forced to abandon their work. In 1975 the Communists conquered the capital and took over the houses.

Anticipating the take-over, Brother Andrew had reluctantly evacuated all the Brothers. However, he chose to stay on, alone. Around him hundreds of thousands of Vietnamese scrambled to leave the country. Hundreds crammed into flimsy fishing vessels and old cargo boats intent on crossing the South China Sea, hoping to find a safe haven elsewhere. Thousands perished at sea, some victims of piracy or hazardous transport. Some "boat people", as they were called by the media, managed to escape and were resettled in America and other countries.

Brother Andrew continued to visit the homes until one by one they were closed by the authorities. Being a foreigner Brother Andrew had to report his movements and activities to the new regime, who eventually demanded his deportation back to India. Leaving Saigon was deeply distressing to him. He wrote: ". . . to be separated so finally from all the people one came to know and love is unbelievably painful. I shall never be the same again after this, and I know that I shall have an ache in my heart for them until the day I die."

Another disappointment was having to bring home a team of Brothers he had sent to another part of east Asia, Cambodia. They were working in similarly dangerous conditions with refugees in the capital Phnom Penh. The Marxist Khmer Rouge were bombing and shelling the capital, determined to take control.

When Brother Andrew asked the Brothers to leave, one young American, Brother Brian Welsh, told him he would stay with the Cambodian people he had grown to love. No amount of persuasion would change his mind, and the Brothers had to evacuate without him. No word was heard of him again, apart from one report of a young American being led away by a soldier at the point of a gun.

In Calcutta, Brother Andrew agonized at the scale of human suffering, at the apparent waste and futility. But as he did the knowledge of God's unchanging goodness brought him renewed comfort and strength. "Have faith in the Lord of History. For there is nothing else that is certain or solid. Everything may collapse, and one may find oneself trapped in some fallen or falling city with all escapes gone . . . Then one would be finally poor – and free. Then one could give one's life and die in peace and love."

With the assurance of God's unfailing presence and help, Brother Andrew supervised the steady expansion of the Brothers' work. In Calcutta a radio training centre was founded for handicapped boys, and four new homes were opened. About fifteen miles outside the city, they purchased Nurpur Farm, where two hundred mentally handicapped boys and men learnt simple farming skills.

The Brothers also worked alongside the Sisters at Kalighat, taking over the running of the men's ward, and at the leprosy centre, Titagarh, where the Sisters handed over the entire work. Medically qualified Brothers cared for three hundred patients and twenty thousand outpatients. Many leprosy sufferers learnt to make rubber flip-flops from worn tyres, to weave sheets and the blue-bordered saris worn by the Sisters.

To enable men to experience a Brother's life without making a definite decision to join, Brother Andrew created "Come and Sees", a term to describe those thinking about becoming a Brother. For a time varying from three to twelve months depending on each individual's needs, young men could share in the Brother's work amongst the poor.

The first "Come and See" was a tall American, Nicholas Prinster, who walked like a cowboy. In fact Nicholas was already a professed Brother, belonging to the Cistercian Order. One day, during a mealtime at his monastery, the story of Mother Teresa's work was read out. Deeply moved, Brother Nicholas, already forty years old, wrote to Mother Teresa and asked if any men were involved in her work.

When Mother Teresa wrote back describing the work of the Brothers, Brother Nicholas asked his Order for permission to go to Calcutta to find out if God really was calling him to a new work. In May 1968 he left his monastery, The Abbey of the Holy Trinity, in the desert of Utah near Salt Lake City, and flew to India.

Brother Nicholas adapted quickly to his new environment and lifestyle, and all was going well until he was suddenly struck down by a bout of fever. As soon as he recovered he was struck down again and, no matter what treatment he received, the fever returned.

Realizing he would have to return to Utah and give up the idea of joining the Brothers, Brother Nicholas's hopes were shattered. However, Brother Andrew believed Brother Nicholas could still serve the Missionaries of Charity Brothers from his monastery. Every time young American men wrote to Brother Andrew, enquiring about becoming a member, he referred them first to Brother Nicholas. One by one, enquirers came to the Abbey in the desert, where they learnt first-hand from Brother Nicholas about the work in Calcutta and took time to pray about their future.

The Abbey also came to represent an important milestone in the history of the Co-Workers movement which was slowly gathering momentum in America. In 1972, Brother Nicholas, with the active support of the head of his Abbey, Abbot Emmanuel, invited the leaders of the American Co-Workers to hold their very first national conference at the monastery. Agreeing to join them for the three-day event, Mother Teresa shared vital principles which eventually led to the rapid growth of the Co-Workers movement in America.

Each day, the Co-Workers, both men and women, joined the thirty-six white-robed monks for early morning communion. Cut off from the consumerism of American society, the Co-Workers were struck by the simplicity and peace of the Abbey and were able to soak up, without distractions, the wise counsel of Mother Teresa.

In order to help the Co-Workers to grasp the importance of doing the work for the right motives, Mother Teresa had many vivid stories to share. She told them about one Brother who came and told her he felt called to serve lepers and lepers alone. She told them: "I said, 'Your vocation, Brother, is not to serve the lepers. It is to belong to Jesus. He has chosen you for Himself; the work is the means to put your love for Christ in action, but your vocation is to belong to Jesus.' He changed completely. Now it doesn't matter whether he is cooking or washing or cleaning the streets or taking care of the lepers. It is 'I belong to Jesus and that is all that matters.'"

Aware of the choking grip of materialism Mother Teresa reminded them: "Here in America you can easily be suffocated by things. And once you have them you must give time for each other or for the poor. You must freely give to the poor what the rich get for their money."

She encouraged them to remember the example of the Cistercians, who, although gifted and cultured, pursued simple activities such as bee-keeping and dairy farming alongside prayer and worship. She also told them: "Love to pray and pray frequently during the day", a habit every Co-Worker tried to follow in their own lives and whenever they met together.

These lessons proved to be secure foundations for a movement that later had the responsibility for handling millions of pounds which were freely donated by American supporters for the work of Mother Teresa.

At the end of the conference Abbot Emmanuel gave Mother Teresa a four-foot-high crucifix as a gift from the Abbey. The Abbot carried the crucifix, which was carefully wrapped in cloth, onto the plane and put it next to Mother Teresa's seat. The steward suggested she would be more comfortable if she took the cross to the first-class section where there were plenty of empty seats. Mother Teresa appreciated the idea and carried the crucifix to the front of the plane. After securing her gift with a safety belt, Mother Teresa returned to her economy-class seat grinning and said, "That's right. We must put Jesus in first class."

Back in Calcutta, as well as "Come and Sees" the Brothers welcomed volunteers, often students, who came for a few months at a time during their summer holidays. The volunteers followed the same routine as the Brothers, getting up at 4.30 a.m., rolling their sleeping mat away and taking a shower with a bucket of water. Like the Sisters, the highlight of each morning was the service of Holy Communion, and only then would they have their breakfast of tea, chappatis and condensed milk.

The volunteers were not spared from helping with the most dire cases. At the Home for the Dying one volunteer described how he cared for a patient whose leg was diseased with gangrene. "A rag was wrapped around it," he wrote, "and we had to take him outside because of the stench. When we washed it down, the water started the blood flowing over the green flesh, bone and muscle dropped off. The foot was no more than a skeleton and you could see right through the leg up to the knee. A crow came down and picked up a bone that had fallen from the foot – they were hungry too."

He went on to relate how the Brothers ate the same lunch and dinner as given out to the poor, often rice and curry, working until 6 p.m. when they gathered together for prayer. The evening meal was eaten in silence apart from a Bible reading, and followed by an hour of fun. "Everyone goes mad, laughs and generally has a good time. It is so obviously a day's release in an hour, as the Brothers are so preoccupied with their work at all other times."

Brother Andrew, after his expulsion from east Asia, went to Los Angeles where he opened a house on "Skid Row", an area which attracted the homeless, alcoholics, tramps , the mentally ill, those often regarded by society as failures. He arrived at a time when a serial killer known as "the Skid Row Slasher" was systematically murdering down-and-outs. It was a full year before the culprit, a tramp, was caught.

The Brothers searched out men who appreciated having someone to chat to, a bath and shave, some new clothes and a hot meal. Many men lived in dingy hotel rooms which were never cleaned or were cluttered with empty bottles.

Sometimes Brother Andrew felt overwhelmed by the vast needs, but like Mother Teresa he recognized the value of caring for each individual. "In God's total plan we need not worry about the numbers we can't reach," he asserted, "we need only be here, love here and believe that the good news of God's love will reach those most crushed, lonely and frightened." Instead of feeling paralysed by all that they could not do, Mother Teresa and Brother Andrew concentrated their energies on what they could do.

Just as the Sisters spread to all corners of the globe, so too did the Brothers, setting up houses in Guatemala, the Philippines, Madagascar, Haiti, Brazil and the Dominican Republic. They also settled in developed countries like Taiwan, Korea, Japan and France, where they helped people who somehow escaped the attention of the welfare services.

In Guatemala, Central America, the Brothers worked alongside the Sisters, surrounded by violence and killing. When Brother Andrew visited them one time, he was struck by their apparent powerlessness. "They are so small and weak and young . . . They care for the old, sick babies, the mothers, the disabled and helpless, the hungry. And they are so full of joy. The light of God shines in their eyes . . . There is no hope here of a solution from arms or politics or ideologies of the Right or the Left. These Sisters and Brothers are so weak, so small. They only have God – His love and His power."

After twenty years' existence, by the end of 1983 there were 302 professed Brothers working in 51 houses in India and overseas. By 1990 this had grown to 380 professed Brothers in 82 houses in 26 countries.

CHAPTER EIGHT

Some years in Mother Teresa's life were particularly eventful. Such a year was 1971, when the country of Bangladesh was struggling for independence from West Pakistan with heart breaking consequences. Ten million refugees were fleeing into India from East Pakistan, attempting to escape the bloody occupation by West Pakistan troops.

Arriving on the doorstep of Calcutta, they merely added to the already over-whelming numbers of the destitute and homeless. Mother Teresa swept into action, enlisting the help of fifteen extra Sisters from outside India who volunteered at a moment's notice. The Indian Government moved rapidly to process passports, relaxing strict rules so that the Sisters could be admitted.

Mother Teresa took over a centre in Green Park, near Calcutta's Dum Dum airport, for child refugees who needed constant care and attention if they were to survive. The scale of the suffering was so vast Mother Teresa made a personal appeal for international help in a booklet that was printed and distributed all over the world.

Let us remember this, (she wrote) the people of Pakistan, the people of India, the people of Vietnam, all people wherever they may be, are the children of God, all created by the same hand. Today the Pakistan refugees belong to us. They are part of God's family in this world. The problem is not only India's problem; it is the world's problem. We have millions of children suffering from malnutrition and starvation. Unless the world comes in with food and proteins, these children will die – and the world will have to answer for their death.

The world responded by sending shiploads and airlifts of food, supplies, lorries, medicine, tents and workers. Mother Teresa and her Sisters chose to work in Salt Lake City, a swampy area originally designated to be a new housing estate but which instead had become an overcrowded refugee camp.

Hundreds of weary, footsore families were huddled into the empty sewer pipes, their shelter from the heavy monsoon rains. Diseases such as cholera, dysentry and smallpox easily took the lives of the already weak and frail. One Sister remembered: "When I picked up dead children, I could hardly feel their weight."

Senator Edward Kennedy, on behalf of the United States Senate, met Mother Teresa and went with her to the centre near Dum Dum airport. He was deeply moved. "You see infants, with their skin hanging loosely in folds from their bones, lacking the strength to lift their heads. You see children with swollen legs and feet, limp in the arms of their mothers. You see babies going blind for lack of vitamins or covered with sores that will not heal. You see in the eyes of their parents, the despair of ever having their children well again. And, most difficult of all, you see the corpse of the child who died just the night before. I have a collection of personal observations that have really burned my soul."

A photograph of Mother Teresa at Salt Lake City cradling an emaciated child in her arms betrayed the agony in her own soul. She also explained later that she felt angry. The suffering of the refugees took a personal toll on Mother Teresa, as she fell ill from utter exhaustion and had to cancel various engagements. However, later that year she was sufficiently recovered to enjoy a personal celebration in Washington.

The year 1971 marked a special anniversary in Mother Teresa's own life. It was twenty-one years since she had set out on her lone mission, and people around the world wanted to recognize the fact by honouring her with two major awards.

On 6th January Pope Paul VI presented her with the Pope John XXIII Peace Award in Rome and eight months later she travelled to

Washington, D.C., to receive a special award from Senator Edward Kennedy, who had so recently seen her work in Calcutta.

The only surviving brother, following the assassination of President John F. Kennedy and Senator Robert Kennedy, Edward Kennedy was the President of a foundation that financed research into mental retardation of children. The foundation wanted to honour those who shared the same convictions and Mother Teresa was a popular choice.

At the award ceremony a clip from the film *Something Beautiful for God* was shown. It was a shot of Mother Teresa holding a tiny baby in her arms. As she looked intently at the child she broke into a beaming smile of pure joy exclaiming, "See! There's life in her!"

Mother Teresa was then presented with a cheque for fifteen thousand dollars and a beautiful cut glass vase. She quickly put the money to good use, investing it in the refugee centre near Dum Dum airport. The centre was renamed The Nirmala Kennedy Centre, and eventually became home to over four hundred handicapped children, many of whom had been abandoned by their parents. The vase was given to the Sisters working in the Bronx, New York, where it took pride of place in their chapel.

Two months later, another immense crisis hit the newly created country of Bangladesh (formerly East Pakistan), and Mother Teresa threw herself into helping the victims. Although the West Pakistan troops had eventually surrendered, they were responsible for the deaths of three million people and it was reported that 200,000 women had been raped.

Mother Teresa and two teams of Sisters were in one of the first convoys of relief lorries to enter Bangladesh. Bishop Ganguly of Dacca gave the Missionaries of Charity a three-hundred-year-old convent, which became a home for some of the rape victims who were pregnant. Fewer of the women came forward for help than had been hoped, out of fear of being identified, as Muslim tradition treated violated women as outcasts.

The leader of the new nation, Sheik Mujibur Rahman, appealed to his people to recognize the sacrifices of these women and to treat them as heroines rather than punish them. Some Freedom Fighters who had fought nobly for their country's liberation offered to marry the "heroines", a brave and costly act. The Sisters also managed to arrange adoptions with people in France, Belgium and Germany for any children who were unwanted.

With the threat of a cholera epidemic, the need for help was urgent and many international agencies joined in the relief efforts. Mother Teresa responded quickly to the immediate problem – "We first had to bury the dead", she explained – but she also identified the longer-term spiritual need. "The greatest need in Bangladesh is for forgiveness. There is so much bitterness and hatred left. Perhaps if they felt loved, they could find it in their hearts to forget what was done to them. I think this is the only thing to bring peace."

As well as the home in Dacca, the Sisters opened clinics providing medicines, vitamins and baby foods. As countless numbers of men had been murdered, many women had been left to fend for themselves. In one village alone, seventeen heads of families had been lined up and shot, and their homes set on fire.

As widows felt ill-equipped to work for a living, many resigned themselves to begging on the streets of Dacca. However, one of the Sisters, Sister Vincentia, had an immensely practical idea: "Every Bengali woman knows how to make puffed rice. With a little help we can start a business."

For minimal cost the Sisters provided the widows with rice, which they prepared at home before selling it at a rented market stall. In this simple but effective way they were able to provide for their fatherless children.

The home in Dacca, once it had outgrown its original purpose, became another Shishu Bhavan, for orphaned and malnourished children. Money for Mother Teresa's work poured in from all over the world, enabling the Sisters to open a Home for the Dying and other centres.

Donations included $20,000 from the monks at the Cistercian Abbey in Utah, who had decided that the work took priority over renovating their own crumbling monastery.

By 1983 the Sisters had given over ten years' uninterrupted service in Bangladesh, when a new law threatened to stop all voluntary donations from overseas. Mother Teresa herself went to Dacca to invite the then President, General Hussein Ershad, to see their Home for the Dying. As soon as he saw their work "He changed", said Mother Teresa , and the Sisters were free to continue receiving the support they needed.

In 1973 five more houses were opened outside India, bringing the total so far to twenty. One of the homes, in Lima, Peru, was in a crowded, noisy shanty town called La Parada, one of the many makeshift housing sprawls that dotted the landscape of the excessively dry and dusty city.

Here Mother Teresa bought a deserted convent which could accommodate at least four hundred people and renamed it "Home of Peace". Soon the peeling pink building was filled with children, the homeless, the elderly, alcoholics and the handicapped. Among the children were two small brothers, Absalom and Ezechiel, who both had disproportionately large heads and walked painfully like fragile old men. The boys were twelve and fourteen years old but continual neglect had stunted their growth and they looked more like six- or seven-year-olds.

A Sister-Nurse had discovered the two boys in a tiny dark house in a mountain village, where they crawled around the dirt floor unable to stand or walk without support. Since their mother had died the father had taken responsibility for them, but he gave them no attention at all, preferring to drink away his money. Close to starving they were sometimes fed by their neighbours, themselves poor.

When the Sister-Nurse asked the father if she could take them to the home in Lima, he readily agreed. Once in the home the boys soon learnt to imitate the other children, copying the way they held their spoon or folded the towels. Although they could not yet talk, their beaming smiles indicated they were proud of each new achievement and keen to make further progress.

The home was surrounded by all kinds of corruption but the Sisters moved about freely, rescuing the dying on the streets or people discharged from hospital with nowhere to go. Reporting to Mother Teresa one Sister wrote: "There are gangs of young thieves who steal wristwatches, purses and carrier bags. Spectacles are torn off noses and the thieves quickly disappear . . . So far, the Sisters have been left in peace.

"Market stalls for shoes, iron, and wood tools

lean against our walls. One can get all kinds of things to eat, not to mention the stalls that sell alcohol, where one or two drunks lie about . . . Once we found a corpse outside the door. So even here, the work is not so different from the work in India. Only the faces, the speech and the customs are different."

Not everyone appreciated the Sisters' presence. One group of priests suggested it would be better if they left, since they were doing nothing to challenge the unjust structures that kept the people in poverty. The Sisters, however, continued to obey their calling, feeding the hungry, caring for the sick, befriending the lonely.

The year 1973 also marked the time when Mother Teresa was given a free Air India pass, which enabled her – at no expense – to travel to all corners of the world. Mother Teresa had in fact once offered to work for the airline as an air hostess on her journeys, in return for free passage. Her offer was politely refused.

The same year Mother Teresa was honoured with a prestigious award, the Templeton Prize for Progress in Religion. The award recognized that her message of love crossed all religious divides and was appreciated by people of every race and creed.

Mother Teresa travelled to England to receive the award, which was presented by Prince

Philip. In her acceptance speech she spoke passionately about Jesus: "Today, as before, when Jesus comes amongst His own, His own don't know Him. He comes in the rotting bodies of the poor. He comes even in the rich who are being suffocated by their riches, in the loneliness of their hearts, and there is no one to love them . . . Jesus comes to you and to me. And often, very often, we pass Him by. Here in England, and in many other places such as Calcutta, we find lonely people who are known only by their addresses, by the number of their room. Where are we, then? Do we really know that there are such people? . . .

"These are the people we must know . . . Let us not be satisfied with just paying money. Money is not enough. Money can be got. They need your hands to serve them. They need your hearts to love them."

A few months after this speech, Mother Teresa with a group of Sisters took the opportunity to put her own words into practice. She travelled to the Yemen Arab Republic, where there were no known Christians but many suffering from the effects of a six-year famine and drought. Although there was no question of building a church, the Sisters were able to show the love of God through their works of compassion, including setting up a home for the mentally ill, clinics, feeding centres and adult education classes.

As well as the home in the Yemen, in 1973 Mother Teresa helped to open homes in Israel, Australia and Ethiopia, and in the following year new homes began in Papua New Guinea, Sicily and Bangladesh. By the autumn of 1975 there were twenty-seven homes outside India, in addition to sixty-one homes within India.

By this time the Missionaries of Charity had been working amongst the poor for twenty-five years and Mother Teresa decided to invite all groups to celebrate the anniversary by services of thanksgiving. Mother Teresa was firm about the arrangements: "Simplicity. No expenses, no concerts, no decorations, only thank you to God. I want God to be the central figure in our celebration so that everybody's attention may be drawn to God and all may acknowledge that it is His work and not ours."

Services were held in different religious buildings all over Calcutta, bringing together Christians, non-Christians and unbelievers. Ten of the original twelve students who first joined Mother Teresa joined in the celebrations, as did the Brothers, Michael Gomes and his family, Archbishop Perier and Father Van Exem. Some of the patients who had survived after being rescued twenty-five years earlier were also able to participate.

Churches around the world, from Lima in

Peru to Amman in Jordan, overflowed with people wanting to express their thanks to God. In Tanzania the elderly and children burst into clapping and began to sing and dance for joy. In New York City a simple-minded man spontaneously and eagerly joined in the offertory procession.

A few weeks later Mother Teresa travelled to the University of North Carolina to receive yet another important award, this time the Albert Schweitzer International Prize. Dr Schweitzer, like Mother Teresa, had devoted his life to the poor, in his case in the inhospitable jungle of Africa.

By the end of 1975 Mother Teresa's face was well known as her picture appeared on the cover of the international journal *Time* magazine. Now aged sixty-five, the picture revealed a care-worn and deeply lined face with small twinkling brown eyes. Under the heading "Living Saints", her story was told, describing her as one through whom the light of God shines.

At an age when most people plan to retire, Mother Teresa still had every intention of carrying on the work. In 1976 six new homes opened, and between 1977 and 1979 thirty-six new homes were established across the globe, ranging from Haiti in the West Indies to Rotterdam in the Netherlands, from Liverpool, England, to Kigali, Rwanda, from Essen in West Germany to Metro-Manila in the Philippines.

Although the rapid expansion of the work meant Mother Teresa could not personally attend every opening, she endeavoured to organise her schedule so that she was available to visit every home at some time. The opening of a home in Mexico City, however, was such a sensitive issue, she went herself to talk to the Mexican President.

President Echeverria was reluctant to advertise to the rest of the world the fact that thousands of his citizens lived in abject poverty, making a risky living from scavenging on the city's burning rubbish tips. However, Mother Teresa reassured him that she admired the creativity and resilience of these people and that she felt her Sisters belonged with them. The President promised to help and provided a van and a plot of land.

The penniless of Mexico City lived on an enormous rubbish tip in a deserted quarry, where richer citizens disposed of ten thousand tons of waste every day. Unintentionally these members of a throwaway society provided endless toil for those willing to endure the filth, stench and fumes. The people who worked there foraged for anything that could be recycled or sold, risking disease and ill-health from the hordes of rats, the burning of old tyres and rotting food.

The workers and their families lived in tiny

huts with corrugated roofs. Often the door was simply a large piece of wood covering a gap in the flimsy wall. Here they kept goats, pigs and chickens to supplement their diet of beans and tortillas. The Sisters visited each home asking about their needs. One reply, "La Palabra de Dios" meaning "the word of God", brought tears of joy to Mother Teresa's eyes.

A multi-purpose centre was built on the land donated by the President, accommodating a convent, a home for the dying, a children's home and a clinic. Abandoned by desperate parents, many children, suffering from blindness, deformed limbs, malnutrition and lung diseases, were cared for by the Sisters.

A large number of Co-Workers aided the Sisters, taking pregnant mothers for hospital appointments, teaching children to read and write, giving personal tuition to adults who wanted to learn to read. One regular visit the Sisters and Co-Workers made together was to Mexico's International Airport, where unwanted in-flight meals were provided free by various airline companies. Rather than waste trays of nourishing food the authorities were happy to see them distributed to those who would probably never have the luxury of using their flying services.

Soon the Sisters were writing about their refuse collectors: "They go through everything.

They pick out things like bottles, broomsticks and cans. There is a special truck that comes to buy them. Our people usually get ten to twenty pesos for their efforts. But when they have big families, and some of them have eight or ten children, it is not possible to buy enough food and clothing. On Sundays, the little church nearby is packed with people."

In Calcutta, Mother Teresa rejoiced at this report and the many others she received from houses all over the world. By the end of 1979 there were one hundred and fifty-eight houses to keep in touch with. Often writing into the small hours of the night, Mother Teresa sent personal messages of encouragement and love to every home.

Before the end of 1979 historic news reached Calcutta that Mother Teresa had been awarded one of the highest honours the world can bestow on any individual, the Nobel Peace Prize. When Mother Teresa heard, her immediate reaction was to visit the chapel to pray.

Her next response was to say, "I am unworthy. Thank God for His gift to the poor." In acknowledging her work Mother Teresa felt the world was also recognizing the value of every poor person. Crowds of supporters and media people turned out to catch a glimpse of Mother Teresa and express their delight. Mother Teresa recalled:

The people began arriving, every type of person, the poor and the richer people. Then the telegrams began coming from President Carter and Senator Kennedy. The one that came from President Reddy (of India) said "You are following closely in the steps of the Prince of Peace". The Sisters said there were more than five hundred telegrams. Every day more letters, sometimes eighty, sometimes more.

To accommodate the overwhelming deluge of mail, a special section was partitioned off at the Calcutta Post Office. It was the first time an Indian citizen had ever been given the award, and a chorus of praise swept around the world.

CHAPTER NINE

On the day that Mother Teresa heard she had been honoured with the Nobel Peace Prize, a tiny abandoned baby was brought to the children's home, Shishu Bhavan. She was named Shanti, meaning Peace, as a tribute to the award and she survived.

"Joy Swept Calcutta" was the headline in the capital's daily newspaper. Journals and papers all around the world echoed their sentiments. The *Washington Post* stated:

> Most of the recipients of the Nobel Peace Prize over the years have been politicians and diplomats. But Mother Teresa, the nun who founded the Missionaries of Charity, has spent the last thirty-one years working with the destitute and dying in Calcutta. It is the example of personal devotion to these people, as individuals, that is compelling . . . Occasionally, the Norwegian Nobel Committee uses the prize to remind the world that there is more than one kind of peace, and that politics is not the only way to pursue it.

As fifty-six candidates had been nominated for the award the announcement that Mother Teresa had received it completely surprised even her closest friends. Unknown to them, the British journalist Malcolm Muggeridge had been keeping in regular correspondence with the Nobel Committee, bringing Mother Teresa's name and work to their attention.

The award ceremony was held at the University of Oslo in Norway on 10th December 1979. An enormous gathering of royalty, dignitaries and nobility applauded vigorously as she accepted the gold peace medal, diploma and a cheque for £95,000.

Facing the distinguished audience Mother Teresa asked them to join her in the beautiful prayer of St Francis of Assisi. For Mother Teresa prayer was as natural as breathing, so although a Nobel audience had never been asked to pray before Mother Teresa did not hesitate. Everyone in the hall echoed these words:

Lord, make me an instrument of Your peace,
Where there is hatred let me sow love, . . .
grant that I may not so much seek to be
    consoled as to console . . .
to be loved as to love,
For it is in giving that we receive;
It is in pardoning that we are pardoned;
and it is in dying that we are born to eternal
    life.

Then without using notes Mother Teresa shared her heartfelt gratitude.

Let us thank God for the opportunity that we all have together today, for this gift of peace that reminds us we have been created to live that peace, and that Jesus became man to bring that good news to the poor. He, being God, became man in all things like us except in sin, and He proclaimed very clearly that He had come to give the good news . . . And God loved the world so much that He gave His Son – it was a giving – it was as if to say it hurt God to give, because He loved the world so much He gave His Son . . it is very important for us to realize that love, to be true, has to hurt.

She then took the opportunity to challenge her audience about their own capacity to love:

Maybe in our own family we have somebody who is feeling lonely, who is feeling sick, who is feeling worried, and these are difficult days for everybody. Are we there? Are we there to receive them? Is the mother there to receive the child?

This led on to a passionate plea for the life of the unborn. Norway had only recently legalized abortion, making it possible for a woman to have an abortion paid for by the state. Totally convinced of the sanctity of human life and regardless of the fact that her words might offend some listeners, Mother Teresa spoke out.

We are talking of peace . . . But I feel the greatest destroyer of peace today is abortion, because it is a direct war, a direct killing, direct murder by the mother herself. And we read in Scripture, for God says very clearly: "Even if a mother could forget her child, I will not forget you. I have carved you in the palm of my hand." We are all carved in the palm of His hand; so close to Him, that unborn child has been carved in the hand of God . . . And today the greatest means – the greatest destroyer of peace – is abortion . . . Because if a mother can kill her own child, what is left but for me to kill you and you to kill me?

She told them how the Missionaries of Charity were fighting abortion with adoption and how they promoted natural family planning.

We are teaching our beggars, our leprosy patients, our slum dwellers, our people of the street, natural family planning. We teach them the temperature method which is very beautiful, very simple. And our poor people understand . . . I think that if our people can do like that, how much more can you do.

Mother Teresa then related some examples of how the poor can teach others about giving, including the moving story of a man who was picked up from the gutter, "half-eaten with worms we brought him to the home. He said gratefully, 'I have lived like an animal in the street, but I am going to die like an angel, loved and cared for.' It was so wonderful to see the greatness of that man who could die like that without blaming anybody, without cursing anybody, without comparing anything. Like an angel – this is the greatness of our people."

She then explained how everyone had their part to play in relieving suffering and misery:

Love begins at home, and it is not how much we do, but how much love we put in the action that we do . . . I want you to find the poor, right here in your own home first. And begin love there. Be that good news to your own people. And find out about your next-door neighbours. Do you know who they are?

Mother Teresa also asked her audience to remember her Sisters, the Brothers and the Co-Workers in prayer.

Pray that we may remain faithful to the gift of God, to love Him and serve Him in the poor together. What we have done we would not have been able to do if you did not share with your prayers, with your gifts, this continual giving. But I don't want you to give from your abundance. I want that you give me until it hurts.

Her central message was one of love:

Let us keep that joy of loving Jesus in our hearts, and share that joy with all that we come in touch with.

Normally after the ceremony there was an elaborate banquet but instead, at Mother Teresa's request, an informal reception was organized. Preferring that the money budgeted for the banquet be given to the poor in Calcutta, she estimated that the banquet costs, three thousand pounds, could feed hundreds of people for a year. This sum, in addition to the award money and donations from the young people of Norway amounting to another £36,000, later provided hundreds of new homes for the street people of Calcutta.

With Mother Teresa for this special occasion were Sister Agnes and Sister Gertrude, the first two young women to accompany her on the streets of Calcutta in 1949. Ann Blaikie from England was there representing the Co-Workers and from Belgium came Jacqueline de Decker, the co-ordinator of the Sick and Suffering Co-

Workers, who could only move with the aid of complicated steel braces. Mother Teresa's brother, Lazar, the only surviving member of her family, had travelled from Sicily for the occasion, with his daughter, Agi, who was now a married woman.

Inevitably the world's press wanted to interview Mother Teresa. Confronted by some one hundred journalists laden with cameras and microphones she answered a barrage of questions. In response to a query as to why she had come to Norway herself to receive the prize she explained: "I am myself unworthy of the prize. I do not want it personally. But by this award the Norwegian people have recognized the existence of the poor. It is on their behalf that I have come."

One persistent journalist managed to draw out from Mother Teresa a particularly memorable statement which gave an insight into her own sense of identity. After remarking that she was born in Yugoslavia and lived in India, while her Sisters worked all over the world, the reporter asked, "And you, Mother Teresa, how do you feel about yourself?"

"By blood and origin," she replied, "I am Albanian. My citizenship is Indian. I am a Catholic nun. As to my calling, I belong to the whole world. As to my heart, I belong entirely to the heart of Jesus."

Newspapers worldwide relayed her words,

and photographs of her featured prominently on countless front pages of national and international magazines. The Norwegian paper *Aftenposten* observed:

> How wonderful to see the world press for once spellbound by a true star, a star without false eyelashes and make-up, without jewels and fur coats, without theatrical gestures. Her joy is the thought of spending the Nobel Prize money for the good of the poorest and the most miserable of the world's people.

For Mother Teresa media attention continued to be a necessary sacrifice. She admitted: "This celebrity has been forced on me. I use it for the love of Jesus. The press makes people aware of the poor, and that is worth any sacrifice on my part." In fact in private Mother Teresa confessed, "For me it is more difficult than bathing a leper."

Whatever the honour, Mother Teresa's main concern was for the glory of God not herself, as she later explained:

> I am not the centre-piece on a prize-giving day. It is Christ using me as His instrument to unite up all the people present. This is what I see happening: people coming to meet each other because of their need for God. I feel that to bring all these people together to talk about

God is really wonderful. A new hope for the world.

Mother Teresa was not without her critics. In India one extreme group published an article entitled "Nothing Noble about Nobel" in which they attacked her motivation. "For when all is said and done", they argued, "she is a missionary. In serving the poor and the sick, her sole objective is to influence people in favour of Christianity and, if possible, to convert them. Missionaries are instruments of Western imperialist countries and not innocent voices of God."

Other opponents from within the Christian Church found fault in Mother Teresa for not attacking the unjust structures that condemned people to a life of poverty. Instead of feeding people they felt she should equip the poor to feed themselves, and to support their argument they quoted the Chinese proverb about giving poor people a fishing rod so they can fish for themselves.

Mother Teresa replied:

Many times they already told me that I must not offer fishes to men, but rods so they can fish themselves! Ah! My God! . . . Our people, so many can't stand. They are hungry, or they are diseased and disabled. Still less are they able to hold the rod. What I do, I give them fish to eat and when they are strong enough, we'll hand them over to you, and you give them the rod to catch the fish.

Mother Teresa did not scorn those who were concerned about social structures but she was clear in her own mind about her own responsibility.

There are in the world those who struggle for justice and for human rights and try to change structures. We are not inattentive to this, but our daily contact is with men who do not even have a piece of bread to eat. Our mission is to look at the problem more individually . . . The very poor do not need words but actions and I have not the conditions to analyse systems, economic patterns, ideologies. I recognize that each person has a conscience and must attend to its calling.

Confident of her own calling Mother Teresa continued her works of compassion and love. Shortly after receiving the Nobel Peace Prize, her adopted country, India, honoured her with its highest civilian award, the Bharat Ratna, the Jewel of India. The first naturalized Indian ever to be presented with it, Mother Teresa accepted the honour at a ceremony in the Presidential Palace, where the President of India announced "She embodies in herself compassion and love of humanity as few in history have done."

India also honoured Mother Teresa by issuing millions of stamps featuring her portrait, the first time such an honour had been given to a nun and to someone who had been born outside India. To celebrate the occasion a special ceremony was held which was televised and broadcast all over India.

Ironically at the same time as her face was appearing on postage stamps around the country, she discovered that the Missionaries of Charity were among a number of voluntary groups banned from starting new projects in West Bengal. The ban, which included Oxfam and the Salvation Army, was designed to prevent aid organizations from showing favouritism towards particular tribal groups.

The story was reported in the *Calcutta Statesman* and quoted Mother Teresa. "All are our brothers and sisters," she said, adding, "If people need us, nothing will stop us." The West Bengal authorities responded promptly with a statement that the Missionaries of Charity were not prohibited from starting new work amongst poor tribal peoples.

One Indian group in another city was not so readily adaptable. Having bought a plot of land for a Home for the Destitute Dying, Mother Teresa found herself at the centre of a major protest campaign organized by many local families. A barrier was built to prevent entry to the building site, and when supporters of Mother Teresa tried to pull it down they were beaten back.

Standing at the barrier Mother Teresa pleaded with the angry crowd, who alleged the home would attract leprosy sufferers. Mother Teresa reassured them that only the homeless and dying would be admitted but they were adamant. The local press carried reports of their fears that the home would decrease the value of their properties and spoil their peace. Mother Teresa could not dissuade them so she decided to abandon the project. "I'm sorry for you people", she said. "Later on you will regret it. You have not rejected me, but you have rejected God's poor."

Failure in one area did not stop the growth of the work elsewhere. By 1980 there were 177 houses. Besides seven new houses in India, the Sisters had set up homes in Papua New Guinea, Nepal, Ethiopia, Belgium, Spain, Chile and Yugoslavia, while the Brothers had moved into Taiwan, Guatemala, Macao and South Korea.

The opening of a House in Zagreb, Yugoslavia, gave Mother Teresa the opportunity to visit her home town of Skopje. It was, however, a very different place from the one she had known as a child. In 1963 a devastating earthquake had destroyed much of the town, including her family home. Looking around the rebuilt city she commented, "It may look completely different, but it is still my Skopje. If there were not so much concrete we could be walking on the pavements of the streets where I spent my childhood." She added, "I am glad to see these places again; at least for a short time I am back in my childhood."

In 1980 a second house was established in Yugoslavia, in Skopje itself. Accompanying her team of Sisters, Mother Teresa said "You gave one person. I bring back four."

They received a warm welcome, and special events were held to honour the return of their most famous daughter. Sister Joselette, who had worked in New York, led the Sisters and confessed that the people were mystified by their lifestyle. She wrote: "We are four Sisters, two Indians, one Maltese, and one Albanian. Our convent is small, just three rooms. We go about everywhere on bicycles. For many material-minded people, we are crazy and funny young ladies. It does not disturb us since we are crazy for the one who was crazy enough to do many more things for us. Only may our craziness spread His glory."

The people they were helping, the old, the blind, the handicapped and the poor, really appreciated their care as revealed in another of Sister Joselette's letters. "We visit all groups including the Gypsies. We go around doing what we can as a sign of God's love. There is so much to say about our people. They are so lovable. Our old people are so beautiful. Many consider us as their daughters . . . We have an old blind woman who takes care of a grandson. She says, 'If it were not for the Sisters, I would never see tomatoes, peppers and all those fresh vegetables and fruits.'"

In the following year, 1981, twenty-six new houses were opened, including East Berlin, Cameroon and Egypt. In May of that year, Mother Teresa celebrated the fiftieth anniversary of her life as a nun, with a Holy Communion service in Calcutta. The next month in New York City another commemorative service was held, when the residents of South Bronx and Harlem gathered together with friends, Sisters, Co-Workers and priests.

An enormous banner proclaiming "Let's Do Something Beautiful for God" welcomed the handicapped, elderly and housebound who had been brought to the service by Sisters and Co-Workers. Men and women in wheelchairs filled the front rows. One of them, a gifted woman, Theoria English, a victim of muscular atrophy, read the Bible lesson from her wheelchair.

Mother Teresa drew close to her handicapped guests when she stood up to speak.

These fifty years have been fifty years of love. Together let us thank God for what He has done, not only through me, but through the Sisters, through the whole society, for the lepers, the dying and the unwanted. We are all the body of Christ. Our faith in Him must prove itself in works. Today I thank the archdiocese for inviting me to come here, and thank all of you for accepting us to work with you."

By this time Mother Teresa was seventy years old, and people had begun to speculate about when she would retire. It was an idea that apparently she had never considered and she soon put a stop to the murmurings when she announced "The poor never retire".

Rather than sit back and reflect on the previous fifty years, Mother Teresa looked ahead to further opportunities to serve her Lord. She did not need to look far. As a result of the Nobel Peace Prize she received a number of requests asking her to carry the message of peace into troubled areas.

One such place was Northern Ireland where she was invited to talk on peace at a Christian festival held in a large tent overlooking the sea, fifty miles north of Belfast. The festival attracted people from both sides of the conflict. Each one knew the heartache of losing a friend or relative through violence. Many felt the separation and pain of having a member of their own family in jail.

Mother Teresa's speech inspired her hearers, including Mairead Corrigan, herself a joint winner of the Nobel Peace Prize in 1976 for her reconciling work in the province. She explained:

Mother Teresa said nothing I had not heard before or read from the gospels, but she brings the whole thing to life. In a gentle but at the same time extraordinarily demanding way, she challenges me to live out personally the Christian life. I think what makes Mother Teresa's words so effective is that she is living out her words in her life. When she tells you that she loves people and she is loved by God, one cannot doubt that fact. Standing on the hill outside the tent (as it was packed) with the gentle rain refreshing me, looking out over the sea, and listening to Mother Teresa saying "God loves you", I felt a deep peace and though tired, felt the desire to rededicate myself and redouble my efforts for peace.

Another peace campaigner, Ciaran McKeown, was also deeply moved. He wrote:

I count 8th July 1981, a day of increasing rain and swirling mist, as the most beautiful day of my life . . . When Mother Teresa indicated that the loving presence of the forgiving God was available to everyone, free, one sensed the immediate truth of it, and this was not the special preserve of persons like herself.

The extraordinary effect was that, when she finished, she had left behind the desire not so much to touch her hand, as happens with other "charismatic" figures, but to speak immediately with the personal God who is so immediately present, and to see and hear God in the persons about, and in the very mist, then sweeping in from the sea.

What greater tribute could there be than to know that your words have drawn others to the love of God?

Mother Teresa's tireless commitment to putting God's love into action also extended to the shell-shocked, war-weary country of Lebanon, where six Sisters had opened a home in the capital, Beirut. Ignoring the potential danger to her own life, Mother Teresa prepared to enter the country. As the main airport had long been closed she embarked on a dangerous seventeen-hour boat trip from the neighbouring island of Cyprus. It was August 1982 and the shelling and bombing were at their worst. It was the first time she had ever gone into an active war zone.

CHAPTER TEN

Arriving in East Beirut, Mother Teresa found her six Sisters safe in spite of constant sniping and gunfire. John de Salis, head of the Red Cross delegation in the Lebanon, told Mother Teresa about a group of mentally ill children who were stranded on the upper floor of a home for the elderly. The home had already been shelled and the children desperately needed fresh water, food and secure shelter.

Privately John de Salis had many reservations about Mother Teresa's ability to help. He later admitted: "At that time I was not clear in my mind of what practical help she could be. We had no water and no power most of the time. We were running out of almost everything. A saint was not what I needed most."

But he could not deny the situation was desperate and little was being done. "The children could be neither fed nor looked after in an area where the chances of bombardment were high. Until Mother Teresa came nobody had been really very keen to take these children." Mother Teresa wasted no time.

She decided the children could be housed with her Sisters, but the acute problem was how to

knew the delicate thoughtfulness of God, such a delicate love."

Such was Mother Teresa's faith in God that she refused to encourage advertising for funds or to accept government funding.

"I don't want the Co-Workers to become a business," she asserted, "but to remain a work of love. I want you to have that complete confidence that God won't let us down. Take Him at His word and seek first the Kingdom of God, and all else will be added on. Joy, peace and unity are more important than money. If God wants me to do something, He gives me the money."

Mother Teresa's convictions also led her to refuse an offer of half a million dollars. A wealthy Indian wanted to bank this money in the Missionaries of Charity's name but there was one condition. "The condition was", explained Mother Teresa , "that this money should not be touched. It should be a security for the work. So, I wrote back and said that rather than offend God, I would offend him a little bit, though I was grateful for his thoughtfulness. I could not accept the money because all these years, God has taken care of us and the security of this money would take away the very life of the work. I could not have money in the bank while people were starving.

"It shocked him. It shook him. Before he died, he sent the money, so much for lepers, so much for the Home for the Dying, so much for food, and so on. He gave it all." She added, "'We must have the courage to say 'No' sometimes."

This courage led the Sisters to remove deep spring mattresses and carpeting from a house in San Francisco that had been donated to the Missionaries of Charity. Mother Teresa had no doubts about the wisdom of her simple lifestyle.

"Many people don't understand why we don't have washing machines, fans, why we don't go to the cinema, to parties. These are natural things and there's nothing wrong with them, but for us we have chosen not to have. For us to be able to understand the poor we must know what is poverty. We accept no government grant, no church maintenance, no salary, no fees, no income as such.

"The flowers, the birds, they don't do anything but God takes care of them. And God takes care of us. We are more important than them."

These convictions also meant she refused all offers of a regular income for the Sisters. One high-ranking churchman once offered five hundred dollars a month for each Sister working in Harlem, New York. Mother Teresa replied, "Do you think God is going to become bankrupt in New York?"

Following the teachings of Jesus, who Himself was poor, Mother Teresa has no doubts about God's ability to provide. "Christ has proved what He said – that we are more important to His Father than the flowers of the field, than the birds of the air and so on. It is really true. We have no income whatsoever, and yet things are just pouring in . . .

"There has not been one single day that we have refused somebody, that we did not have food, that we did not have a bed or something, and we deal with thousands of people. We have 53,000 lepers and yet never one has been sent away because we did not have. It is always there although we have no salaries. We receive freely and give freely. This has been such a beautiful gift of God."

God's ability to provide against seemingly impossible odds was clearly demonstrated when Mother Teresa visited Ethiopia to investigate the possibility of reaching out to the poor in the drought-stricken north. Most relief workers thought it would be impossible to gain permission for the Sisters to enter the country. However, with great difficulty a meeting was arranged with Emperor Haile Selassie's daughter.

The Princess, genuinely interested in the work of the Missionaries of Charity, arranged for Mother Teresa to meet her father the following day. Before the royal interview a Minister of the Imperial Court asked Mother Teresa various strategic questions.

"What do you want from the Government?"

"Nothing", replied Mother Teresa , "I have

only come to offer my Sisters to work among the poor suffering people."

"What will your Sisters do?"

"We give wholehearted free service to the poorest of the poor."

"What qualifications do they have?"

"We try to bring tender love and compassion to the unwanted and the unloved."

"I see you have quite a different approach. Do you preach to the people, trying to convert them?"

"Our works of love reveal to the suffering poor the love of God for them."

Mother Teresa was then escorted into the presence of the eighty-year-old Emperor. The meeting was brief and the outcome entirely surprising and unexpected. "I have heard about the good work you do. I am very happy you have come. Yes, let your Sisters come to Ethiopia."

Mother Teresa left behind a Sister to find a suitable house in the capital, Addis Ababa, and God again provided in a miraculous way. She described her search. "I came across two houses that had the sign 'To Let' on the window and was very near concluding the contract for one of the houses at a rent of 250 Ethiopian dollars a month, when I decided to wait another day. Next morning I went out on my usual tour, taking a different direction. I spotted another house with the notice 'To Let'."

When the Sister spoke to the landlord at first he quoted a rent of 450 Ethiopian dollars. Eventually he gave the Missionaries of Charity the use of the property for no charge at all!

Such stories are not confined to the Third World or to members of the Order. A Co-Worker recalls one Christmas when the usual supply of food had not been given to the London home for the tramps' annual Christmas party. Unwilling to use money which had been set aside for other needs, the worker prayed.

Next morning the first letter she opened contained a cheque for £1,000 from someone who specifically asked that the money be put towards a party for the city's down-and-outs.

The importance of prayer to Mother Teresa and her work cannot be over-estimated. For Mother Teresa to pray is to have a living dialogue with her loving Lord. "This is the community's greatest treasure, and we derive our strength from it."

Prayer was something she learnt as a child from her family. She recalled: "I remember my mother, my father and the rest of us praying together each evening . . . I hope our Albanian families have remained faithful to this practice. It is God's greatest gift to the family. It maintains family unity. The family that does not pray together does not stay together . . . Through prayer you will find what God wants you to do."

Prayer is absolutely vital in all circumstances and is not confined to the daily prayer times with her Sisters. Mother Teresa says, "Love to pray – feel often during the day the need for prayer and take trouble to pray. Prayer enlarges the heart until it is capable of containing God's gift. Ask and seek, and your heart will grow big enough to receive Him and keep Him as your own."

Prayer may also be silent. "We need to find God and He cannot be found in noise and restlessness. God is the friend of silence. See how nature – trees, flowers, grass – grows in silence. Is not our mission to give God to the poor in the slums? Not a dead God, but a living, loving God.

"The more we receive in silent prayer, the more we can give in active life. We need silence to be able to touch souls. The essential thing is not what we say, but what God says to us and through us. All our words will be useless unless they come from within – words which do not give the light of Christ increase the darkness."

This dialogue with God can continue in all time and in all places. "You can pray while you work. Work doesn't stop prayer, and prayer doesn't stop work. It requires only that small raising of mind to Him. 'I love you, God, I trust You, I believe in You, I need You now.' Small things like that. They are wonderful prayers."

In September 1974 Mother Teresa asked a French priest and Chairman of the French Co-Workers, Father Georges Gorrée, to organize an international prayer programme. It had long been her wish to see each of her Houses "spiritually adopted" by one or more contemplative communities of other Orders throughout the world. Her hope was that these praying groups would enable the work of the Missionaries of Charity to be even more effective and fruitful.

Father Gorrée agreed to put the scheme into operation. After the first twelve months he was able to report, "In just one year, about four hundred convents in Germany, England, Belgium, Canada, Spain, France, Italy and Luxembourg have enthusiastically accepted this spiritual twinning. This is marvellous! Unique! Many of the Missionaries of Charity have written to me to say how happy they are at the thought of their contemplative Sisters offering their prayers and sacrifices for them . . ."

Each convent promised to pray daily for their allotted House, and even after Father Gorrée's death the idea spread to other countries such as Poland, and included Anglican communities. The task of continuing the scheme was handed on to Sister Nirmala, and one day she received a letter which highlighted the crucial part prayer had played ever since Mother Teresa had stepped out into the streets of Calcutta.

The letter came from the prioress of a Carmelite monastery in the United States and revealed that while Mother Teresa was waiting for permission from the Pope to begin her new work, her superior had written to a Sister there asking for prayers for the project.

The prioress wrote, "Ever since that day in the 1940s we have been praying for Mother Teresa and for her work, following with loving, apostolic interest each new development that Providence permitted us to hear about. We were linked with your Order since the time there were four members, all unknown to any of you, but hopefully supporting all of you. This we will continue to do, putting special emphasis on the Missionaries of Charity in Silchar, India."

Among Mother Teresa's Sisters there were those who wished to devote themselves to prayer, so in 1976 Mother Teresa established a new branch of the Order, the Contemplative Missionaries of Charity, to be known as the Sisters of the Word. Sister Nirmala became Superior of the first House, which opened in the troubled Bronx area of New York.

Although more time was to be spent in prayer the Sisters' day also included several hours' work each afternoon amongst the local poor. The Sisters in New York took over an empty church, which was also made available to lay people who wanted to pray. The Sisters would spend two hours each day visiting patients in hospital and the housebound. Their deep prayer life was to be worked out in active service.

Sister Nirmala reported, "People are frightened to come where we are and yet the Lord has chosen this place for us and it is the right place, as here we have the most needy – people broken in spirit."

Sometimes there was opposition, as experienced by Sister Nirmala one day as she prayed in a nearby park. She was approached by a young man pointing the blade of a penknife at her. As he stood threatening her, other Sisters arrived and gathered round. They began to pray and as he listened the man put his knife away. When they started to sing Psalm 19 he joined in. Afterwards he said, "I will protect you in this park as if I am the guardian angel of the place."

A second house was opened in Brooklyn, New York, the third in a run-down area of Washington, D.C. Soon after the Contemplative Sisters were founded Mother Teresa began a similar branch for men. From their house in Rome, a Missionary Brother of the Word described the people they were able to help in the two or three hours allocated to helping the poor.

"Following the example of Jesus Christ the Good Shepherd, we go out to seek the lost sheep to proclaim the Good News: to the alcoholics and drug addicts wherever they may be found; to the lonely and the aged; to the prisoners – to encourage them to seek mercy and forgiveness from God; to pray with the men at a night shelter; to encourage the downhearted . . . in a word to be available to anyone who is in most need of spiritual and material help . . ."

By 1980 the Contemplative Sister and Brothers were intrinsically linked with the Sisters and Brothers of the Missionaries of Charity. Quietly in the background the Co-Workers maintained their practical and prayerful support as they pursued the ordinary affairs of everyday life.

Inspired by Mother Teresa's vision, and concerned about the dwindling enthusiasm for joining the priesthood, a number of priests suggested a group of Priest Co-Workers be formed. Although not free to join the Brotherhood they wanted to be as closely identified with the Missionaries of Charity as possible.

Mother Teresa replied by asking them to wait on God and to pray. A year later the priests repeated their request and Mother Teresa presented the idea to Pope John Paul II for his approval.

The Pope responded with unprecedented support, saying "Mother Teresa, allow me to be the first priest to be accepted into this community of Co-Workers of Mother Teresa." On 26th June 1981 the new branch of Co-Workers was officially recognized and Mother Teresa asked a young American priest, Father Joseph Langford, to head the movement. So the Missionaries of Charity entered the eighties and looked ahead to even greater challenges.

CHAPTER ELEVEN

The year 1981 also marked the year when Mother Teresa heard the news that her natural brother, Lazar, had died. She wrote, "One person who must have been longing for him to join the family was, I am sure, my mother. Her only son, whom she loved more than her life, is at last with her. He died a beautiful death – it was really going home to God."

Two years later, early in June 1983, people feared that Mother Teresa herself, almost seventy-three years old, was about to meet her Lord. Whilst visiting some Sisters in Rome she had a minor accident which proved to be a blessing in disguise as Mother Teresa herself explained.

"What happened was, I fell out of bed . . . I felt a pain in my side. I thought I ought to go to hospital because something might be broken. They took X-rays. The doctor said that there was no fracture, but there was something the matter with my heart . . .

"They told me that if the fall had not made me come to the hospital, I would have had a heart attack. There was no reason for falling. See the wonderful ways of God! Saint Peter must have said, 'Hold her back there. There are no slums in heaven.'

"Then I got letters and telegrams. I never realized that people loved the poor so much . . . I received a card from Yemen from the President. President Singh of India telegraphed, and a telegram came from President Reagan; he signed it from himself and Nancy.

"Sisters were praying, and all the Co-Workers, and all the other people I don't know – what a great amount of prayers going to God. That was the wonderful thing; that's what the world needs."

Whilst in hospital Mother Teresa asked for pen and paper to write down her meditations on the subject "Who is Jesus to me". She shared her thoughts with the Sisters who in turn shared them with the co-Workers. She wrote:

The Word made flesh
The Bread of Life
The Victim offered for our sins on the cross . . .
The Way to be walked
The Joy to be shared
The Peace to be given . . .

Using less familiar expressions she described Jesus in His distressing disguise.

The Leper – to wash His wounds.
The Beggar – to give Him a smile.
The Drunkard – to listen to Him.

The Mental – to protect Him.
The Little One – to embrace Him.
The Blind – to lead Him.
The Dumb – to speak for Him.
The Crippled – to walk with Him.
The Drug Addict – to befriend Him.
The Prostitute – to remove from danger and befriend her.
The Prisoner – to be visited.
The Old – to be served.

She finished with the words:

To me, Jesus is my God
    Jesus is my Spouse
    Jesus is my Life
    Jesus is my only Love
    Jesus is my all in all.
    Jesus is my everything.

Jesus I love with all my heart,
with my whole being.
I have given Him all, even my sins,
and He has espoused me to Himself in tenderness and love.
Now and for life
I am the spouse of my crucified Spouse. Amen.

In less than seven weeks Mother Teresa was back at work, visiting the Sisters in New York. Shortly afterwards she was invited to Poland to establish a House in Warsaw. En route she visited her Sisters in East Germany, which at that time was a Communist stronghold, and discussed the opening of a second house in the country.

Six months after her illness Mother Teresa was summoned to Delhi to accept an Honorary Order of Merit, the highest possible British award. She was presented with the award by Queen Elizabeth II who was on a state visit to the country. The award can only be held by twenty-four people at any one time.

The expansion of the society continued at a rapid pace. By the end of 1984 there were 2,400 Sisters, working in 270 Houses around the world, including 120 in India. In addition there were 70 Houses of the Brothers. During the year Mother Teresa visited as many Houses in India as she could. She continued to join in the daily chores and invariably chose to clean the bathroom.

Two additional groups were added to "Mother Teresa's family" in 1984, one, the Medical Co-Workers, which united medical personnel around the world who wished to practise their profession in the spirit of Mother Teresa and the Missionaries of Charity. The new group was not just for doctors who donated their services wherever in the world there was a need. It also included doctors who were concerned to develop a truly compassionate and caring relationship with their patients.

The other group was separate from the Co-Workers, the movement of the Carriers of God's Love. For some time young women had expressed a desire to live a life similar to that of the Missionaries of Charity but without becoming Sisters. Some Christian women were not free to join the Order but wanted to adopt the same life of simplicity, purity and service as practised by the Sisters. Women from many different religious and cultural backgrounds united together to express an ever-deepening commitment to reaching the most vulnerable in society, the poorest of the poor.

A request from the Pope also took her to Rome in April 1984, where she addressed a world rally of Catholic youth in St Peter's Square and the Colosseum. Six month later she returned to speak to 6,500 priests. Her words were simultaneously translated into several languages, for the priests came from all corners of the globe.

For a woman to address priests as Mother Teresa did was a remarkable event for a body which traditionally does not give women an important role in the church. Joseph Langford, head of the Priest Co-Workers, observed many priests were close to tears. Her message was simple, "Be Holy, like Jesus."

One outcome of the gathering was that Mother Teresa was asked to support the formation of a congregation of priests whose primary function was to pray for the work of the Missionaries of Charity. The new society was born and became known as the Missionary Fathers of Charity. At the time Mother Teresa remarked, "I don't think I will start anything more."

Towards the end of 1984 Mother Teresa's beloved India was torn apart by violence. Her friend, Prime Minister Indira Gandhi, was killed by two of her own bodyguards who were members of the Sikh community. Revenge attacks on Sikh people followed, leaving hundreds dead.

Mother Teresa took teams of her Sisters into the refugee camps where Sikhs had fled for safety. Frail and stooped, Mother Teresa gave no thought to her own needs, and tended the bereaved and orphaned, reassuring them with the words, "We must love one another, that is all Jesus came to tell us."

The following month India suffered another agony in the spectre of a toxic gas leak in the city of Bhopal, four hundred miles south of Delhi. The cloud of poison seeped through a shanty town killing hundreds as they slept. Over two and a half thousand people died in a few days, and more than one hundred thousand suffered serious damage to their lungs and eyes. A Missionaries of Charity team who had been working in Bhopal for many years escaped death because the wind blew the gas in another direction.

Mother Teresa rushed to the scene to assist her Sisters, who were already helping where they could. It was one of the world's worst industrial accidents, and clearly there would be plenty of work for the Sisters to do in the years ahead.

The following year Mother Teresa visited another disaster area, Ethiopia, where famine threatened the lives of millions of people. Her visit was televised and Mother Teresa made good use of the publicity. Standing in front of television cameras, she asked a government minister if a building she had seen was available to set up as an orphanage. With the world looking on he could hardly refuse!

By 1985 a small team of Sisters had taken on the task of visiting Houses overseas on behalf of Mother Teresa. However, there were some projects that Mother Teresa chose to visit herself. One such project was an AIDS mission in New York's Greenwich Village.

Determined to respond to all needs, Mother Teresa called on New York's Mayor Ed Koch and told him she wanted to open a hospice for infants with AIDS. The Mayor, in response, pleaded for Mother Teresa to help adult sufferers, as they were often victims of fierce and unforgiving condemnation. He reasoned, "Nobody is going to take on Mother Teresa, whatever she wants to do."

The Mayor's plea resulted in a new 15-bed

hospice for adults, "the Gift of Love", which opened on Christmas Eve 1985. Many of the patients were young men, who often arrived angry and embittered. The Sisters, led by Sister Sabita, helped many to find new hope and faith. The House itself was imaginatively organized to foster good relations. Deliberately there was no television. "We want them to talk to each other, develop a sense of community, not be lost in television", said Sister Sabita. The hospice made an immediate impact, and only ten months later forty prisoners suffering with AIDS were transferred to the hospice.

Another remarkable development occurred in 1986, when Mother Teresa, on a visit to Cuba, persuaded the communist President, Fidel Castro, to allow her Order to establish a mission in Havana. For years the country had prided itself on eradicating material poverty and suppressing religious observance. By inviting Mother Teresa to work in the country they were acknowledging the worth of helping others inspired by spiritual values.

Shortly after her visit to Cuba, Mother Teresa travelled to another communist stronghold, East Berlin, to pray with nuns at one of her houses in the city. Crossing over to West Germany, she met with Chancellor Kohl at his home, and joined in a prayer march organized by an anti-abortion group.

A few months later, in October 1986, Mother

Teresa embarked on a tour of East Africa which ended in tragedy. As the light aircraft in which she was travelling prepared for take-off on a makeshift runway near Dodoma, in central Tanzania, it slewed off the runway. Out of control, the plane careered into a crowd of onlookers killing five people. Two boys, Sister Serena (an Indian missionary nun), the director of a leprosy centre and another Tanzanian man died.

Mother Teresa was deeply saddened by the accident and was tempted to abandon the rest of the tour. However, after attending the funeral of Sister Serena she decided to continue and flew to Tabora, western Tanzania, where she attended a ceremony at which seven members of the Order took their first vows.

Following on from her success in Cuba, Mother Teresa made a highly publicized visit to the Soviet Union and offered the services of four of her nuns. Like Cuba, the country once prided itself on providing for all equally, without religious support. However, disillusionment with Communist ideologies and large scale corruption had persuaded the authorities to encourage and welcome voluntary and charitable works.

On the five-day visit Mother Teresa visited a newly-built housing project for victims of the Chernobyl nuclear disaster. Careful to avoid making any political remarks Mother Teresa did say she had been trying for many years to come to the country and was overjoyed when the Soviet Peace Committee invited her.

Speaking without notes, she urged listeners to recover lost values of faith, charity and love. Such sentiments were rarely acknowledged in public, and they made a visible impact on the dignitaries accompanying her.

Back in the Western world, Mother Teresa still managed to capture the headlines. In August 1987 she paid an unexpected visit to the Gift of Love in New York. Her surprise arrival caused a minor commotion. In spite of her weak heart she climbed to the third floor and spoke to one of the patients, Juan, who was close to death. Juan looked at Mother Teresa and smiled as they clasped hands.

Mother Teresa had a poignant message for him. "When you get to Jesus, Juan, tell him that I love you, that the Sisters, the volunteers and the patients love you. He will know that you have much love. Keep smiling."

As she left the building Mother Teresa noticed a "For sale" sign on the house next to the Gift of Love. She knelt in front of the building and prayed. Rising to her feet she told her companion, "We could care for 15 or 20 more . . . Those buildings are right together . . . it would be so beautiful. If God wants us to have it, he will make it possible."

Risking criticism and cynicism Mother Teresa

defended her work with AIDS victims saying, "We are not here to sit in judgement on these people, to decide guilt or blame. Our mission is to help them make their dying days more tolerable, and we have Sisters who are dedicated to do that."

On 27th August 1987 Mother Teresa celebrated her seventy-seventh birthday. She happened to be in north London where she was making a flying visit to her Sisters in Kilburn. Over one hundred homeless men had gathered in a church hall for soup when the tiny figure of Mother Teresa appeared. Speaking in a firm voice she told them: "God loves you ALL." Everyone joined in together singing "Happy Birthday dear MOTHER . . ."

Inevitably people again wondered when Mother Teresa would give up work. Questioned by an interviewer one of the Sisters reported, "Mother said, she wants to die on her feet and I think that's what she's doing. Giving herself to the last drop."

Certainly if Mother Teresa's plans were anything to go by, she had no intention of giving up work. Early in 1988 she announced plans to set up houses in China, the former Soviet Union and South Africa, and she determined to visit the countries herself.

Returning to London in April 1988 Mother Teresa pricked the nation's conscience when she drew attention to the plight of the capital's homeless. After making a late night tour of Lincoln's Inn Fields, the Temple Gardens and the railway arches behind Embankment Station, she was moved to tears. "It hurt me so much to see our people in the terrible cold with just a bit of cardboard covering them. They were inside that cardboard box made like a little coffin. I didn't know what to say . . . my eyes were full of tears." It was characteristic of Mother Teresa to use the phrase "our people" – the poor are always "we" to her.

"There was this man lying there protecting himself from the cold with no home and no hope. He looked up and said: 'It is a long long time since I felt the warmth of a human hand.' It was very painful and sad to see him and many other people like him. They are unwanted, unloved and uncared for."

At a half-hour meeting with the Prime Minister, Margaret Thatcher, Mother Teresa appealed for help to set up a new hostel for the elderly homeless. The next year, however, without naming the Prime Minister, she admitted to disappointment in an interview with a women's magazine: "I talked to the highest people but nothing has happened. A number of people promised to do something but we have no home. That is what worries me sometimes – the feeling of helplessness. I wonder what I have to do to get things done."

During her stay Mother Teresa also went to

the House of Commons to campaign against abortion. She appealed to MPs, in vain, to support David Alton's Bill to reduce the time limit for abortions to eighteen weeks. Another disappointment followed, this time personal. A few months later in July she was forced to cancel a visit to New Zealand and Australia as she had to have eye surgery in New York.

In spite of these setbacks Mother Teresa persevered. At the end of 1988, when a large-scale earthquake devastated Armenia in the Soviet Union, she flew there with a group of nuns to offer help to the survivors. The following year she became the first known Christian dignitary to visit Albania, the world's first atheist state. After a "cultural" revolution in 1967 all religious buildings were destroyed, and everyone known to have religious beliefs was killed, imprisoned or forced into hiding.

The occasion was particularly memorable for Mother Teresa as her own parents had been Albanian. As a result of her visit her Order became the first religious body to be allowed to operate openly with the government's full approval.

In September 1989 Mother Teresa returned to hospital with chest pains, but within three weeks she was back at work. However, three months later she was readmitted to hospital suffering from severe giddiness. Doctors inserted a heart pacemaker and a few days later she was discharged.

With a new lease of life Mother Teresa moved into the nineties. In May 1990 she made her first visit to Romania, where a harsh repressive regime had been responsible for neglecting thousands of babies and children, as well as severe persecution of the Christian Church.

By the end of the year there were over three thousand Sisters, some four hundred Brothers, over one hundred and thirty thousand Co-Workers, nearly two hundred homes for the mentally ill and abandoned children, over four hundred and fifty feeding centres, and some one thousand mobile clinics.

Now in her eightieth year, Mother Teresa understandably began to think about the appointment of someone else as Mother Superior of the Order she had founded. She first asked the Vatican for permission to step down as head of the Order, which was granted. A conclave of Sisters was convened to elect a successor in a secret ballot. However, there was no clear choice so she had to seek approval to reassume leadership.

In 1991, nearly two years after her original visit to Albania, she returned to the country with four nuns to open a House in the capital city, Tirana. After mass public demonstrations the law forbidding religious activity had been relaxed, allowing churches and mosques to reopen. The media headlines described her as "Albania's most famous daughter".

Mother Teresa was delighted to be able to take the good news of Jesus to people who had been denied the opportunity to hear about Him for many years. She wrote, "Glory and honour to God for all He has done for us in Albania where the people are so hungry for God . . . We have opened the Cathedral Church of the Sacred Heart in Tirana which all these years was used as a cinema hall."

Two months later she travelled to an equally notorious country, Iraq, at the invitation of Saddam Hussein's government. She was able to take with her five Sisters to open a House which was soon filled with under-nourished and disabled children. Mother Teresa, well aware that her visit signified an amazing success, commented, "It is a real living miracle of God's tender love for His suffering children that we were allowed by the government of Iraq to have the Missionaries of Charity House in the heart of Baghdad."

By the end of 1991 the Order was established in 95 countries, and there seemed little sign of Mother Teresa slowing down. But whilst in Mexico celebrating Christmas at the Missionaries of Charity home in the border town of Tijuana, she was taken ill again. A cold and cough developed into pneumonia, causing her to be hospitalized in the Scripps Clinic and

Research Foundation in La Jolla, California.

The Californian doctors decided to use sophisticated surgery so that blood could reach the heart muscle which had been weakened by lack of oxygen. The specialized operation was a complete success and Mother Teresa was able to leave hospital after three weeks. During that time she celebrated her sixty-third anniversary as a nun.

Although she had not fully recovered, Mother Teresa was given permission to travel because her health had greatly improved. On her return journey to Calcutta, Mother Teresa stopped in Rome for a private audience with the Pope. An Italian newspaper reported that she was in a hurry to be back in Calcutta. "Charity doesn't wait, especially now we have been allowed to open our first mission in China", she said.

Mother Teresa's hope, however, was a little premature as she unexpectedly suffered an angina attack which prevented her from continuing her journey.

CHAPTER TWELVE

Falling ill in Rome was not only a setack for
Mother Teresa but it was also a disappointment
for the Princess of Wales. On the last day of her
official visit to India with the Prince of Wales,
the Princess visited the children's home Shishu
Bhavan in Calcutta, and discovered that Mother
Teresa was unable to meet her. The Princess was
so eager to keep the appointment that she
rescheduled her return flight via Rome, where
Mother Teresa had just been discharged from
the clinic after an angina attack. Together for the
first time, a smiling Mother Teresa and the
Princess hugged and kissed one another.

They met in the garden of the simple convent
of the Missionaries of Mercy of Calcutta, where
nuns had placed a blackboard which read
"Welcome dearest Princess". The Princess and
Mother Teresa spent twenty minutes in private
conversation together, then they walked to the
chapel inside the convent. After removing their
shoes before going inside, they knelt at the altar
and prayed together for a few minutes.

They embraced again at the door of the
chapel, then Mother Teresa introduced the
Princess to several of the Sisters. The Princess

asked after Mother Teresa's health and congratulated the nun who had looked after her the most, saying: "I'm happy you've got her back on her feet." Immediately after the visit the Princess flew back to London and Mother Teresa prepared to fly to Calcutta.

The Princess of Wales joins a long list of people all over the world who have personally met Mother Teresa. Rich or poor, famous or unknown, each one has their own story and unforgettable memory.

During Christmas 1975 Cliff Richard led her staff in an impromptu and unique hour of carol and chorus singing in the cobbled courtyard of their Home for the Destitute and Dying. After meeting Mother Teresa, Cliff wrote in his autobiography "I've never met a more Jesus-centred person."

In 1985 she joined the Live Aid campaign for famine relief in Africa and met its organizer, Bob Geldof, in Ethiopia. He wrote "The second I met Mother Teresa she struck me as being the living embodiment of moral good. I felt I had no business sitting beside this tiny giant. There was no false modesty about her and there was certainty of purpose which left her little patience. But she was totally selfless; every moment her aim seemed to be, how can I use this or that situation to help others. She was never pious about this . . . She is one of the few people who have impressed me on sight. I was in awe of her."

Similarly the Prime Minister of India, Indira Gandhi, wrote, "To meet her is to feel utterly humble, to sense the power of tenderness, the strength of love."

Mother Teresa also made an impact when appearing live on Spanish television. She left her experienced, well-known interviewer speechless when she finished the programme by leading everyone in prayer.

Shortly after being received into the Catholic Church at the age of seventy-nine, broadcaster and journalist Malcolm Muggeridge said: "She has given me a whole new vision of what being a Christian means; of the amazing power of love, and how in one dedicated soul it can burgeon to cover the whole world."

After Garth Hewitt, one of Britain's best-known Christian singers, met her he was inspired to write a song. He explained, "As we talked together Mother Teresa described her work among the destitute and the dying in a memorable phrase: she spoke of giving 'dignity to the poor'. It was a phrase that was to stick strongly in my mind." The phrase eventually developed into the theme of his song *Road to Freedom*.

Less well-known figures have also been deeply challenged. After meeting Mother Teresa in Pakistan a British missionary, Mary Parish, wrote: "I was fascinated by her humour, iron spirit, and transparent gentleness – and her talking to a roomful of diplomats about prayer, and service, and holiness. She was wonderful.

"I felt it a great privilege to be almost the only person in the room who was doing, even in a small way, what is so close to her own heart – serving the poor. 'Lord, make us worthy', she prayed, 'to serve the poor.' I was moved: so often we feel we must be worthy to serve the rich and influential!

"She had been with people all day including Nawaz Sharif [the Prime Minister of Pakistan] yet was still so open and receptive to everyone. At the end of her time she went for her 'one hour of prayer'. 'Whatever she is doing,' I was told, 'she must have her one hour of prayer!' So that's how she manages it all . . . What a challenge."

One Christian family, living in Belgium, who already had two children of their own, were deeply challenged by Mother Teresa's commitment to "adoption not abortion". Through her adoption scheme they adopted, over a number of years, twenty-four orphans. These children, some of whom were severely disabled, came from places as diverse as Vietnam, Korea, India, Haiti, Cambodia and Guatemala.

There are also thousands of men and women who have radically changed their lives because of her example, becoming lifelong members of the Order. Sister Premila is typical of such people, renouncing a comfortable life in order to serve the poor.

Sister Premila had been brought up in Mangalore in South India, a tranquil and lovely place where poverty was relatively inconspicuous. Her goal was to teach "in the best of schools because they give you the best money and have the best students." After seeing something of Mother Teresa's work her future plans were turned upside down.

". . . I found I had a great desire to do something but I didn't know what, until I visited a school run by Mother Teresa and I was taken aback. It was in the heart of a slum and because it was the rainy season the whole place was flooded. The houses were just three feet square. made with four poles and rags and things, and whole families were living in them. Right in the middle of the slum they had built a school, exactly like the structures the people were living in, only a little bigger. There were a hundred children . . . I was deepy moved because in our proper schools we are so fastidious about equipment and surroundings. I thought, here I was, a qualified teacher, doing what? . . . when I met Mother I wanted to be a volunteer but she asked me if I would not like to join her. For ever. And I did."

Mother Teresa's life and words have also made an impact on countless others who have never met her and are likely never to. A young French couple wrote: "We will be married in a month. We have asked our relatives and friends that instead of getting gifts for us, they give the amount they would have spent to Mother Teresa's poor. We want to have a small intimate wedding without uselessly spending money."

Similarly children have responded to her example by wanting to be involved in her work. For many years children in Denmark have regularly paid for shipments of powdered milk and vitamin pills to India. Every week school-children in Spain give up some of their pocket money for Mother Teresa's work.

The most precious stories concern the poor themselves. Ann Blaikie, chairman of the Co-Workers, recalled the following incident. "One day as we were walking with Mother Teresa along the streets of Calcutta, a young man dashed up to us and knelt down to kiss Mother Teresa's feet. He told her that he was going to be married in a few hours' time. Mother Teresa explained to me that, a few months before, the young man had been brought dying from hunger and tuberculosis, to the Home of the Dying. At the house he had been cared for and he had learnt a modest occupation, shining shoes. It had been enough to enable him to start a new life."

Mother Teresa herself tells of the day she met a beggar who gave her everything he had. "Everybody gives you something," he said, "and I'm going to also – in fact, everything I have."

"That day," Mother Teresa says, "the beggar had received but one bolivar (a small coin). He gave it to me and said: 'Take it, Mother Teresa, for your poor.'"

Mother Teresa was deeply moved. "In my heart I felt that the poor man had given me more than the Nobel Prize because he gave me all he had. In all probability, no one gave him anything else that night and he went to bed hungry."

In the early days of her work on the streets Mother Teresa visited a family living in the slumbs of Mohti Jihl in Calcutta. As a result of her visit, the life of their teenage daughter Agnes changed beyond all recognition.

The family lived in a tiny house with just enough room for two beds, a number of boxes, a small stove and some cooking utensils. Agnes shared this home with her parents, three sisters and three brothers. The children had all attended the Mohti Jihl school, where the provision of a daily glass of milk and other foods had enabled the family to survive.

The mother had sent for Mother Teresa because her fourteen-year-old daughter, Shurji, felt so overwhelmed by the poverty around her she could only sit huddled inside her home. Mother Teresa arranged for Shurji to move to Shishu Bhavan where she studied and helped with the smaller children.

Agnes, who earned some money working as a

cook and dishwasher, never forgot how Mother Teresa rescued her sister. Years later she trained to be a nurse under two of Mother Teresa's Sisters, and eventually took charge of the leprosy centre at Dhappa. Here Agnes cared for leprosy sufferers who were so disabled, with fingers or feet half-eaten away or gutted eye sockets, that they were unable to beg or feed themselves. Agnes also chose not to marry, an unheard-of decision for a Hindu girl but acceptable to a Christian community.

Clearly many people hold Mother Teresa in the highest esteem, so much so that she has been asked on more than one occasion what it feels like to be a living saint. Mother Teresa, however, has no illusions of grandeur. When this question was put to her by one press reporter she replied, "I'm very happy if you can see Jesus in me, because I can see Jesus in you. Holiness is not just for a few people. It's for everyone, including you, sir."

As well as being genuinely humble she has always been eager to divert praise away from herself to God. When asked how she inspired her former students to join her in the early days of her work, she remarked, "The love the student had for me and the influence I had over them for good – it was nothing I could take pride in. It was God using me."

Some commentators have tried to give the impression that Mother Teresa's work was merely a human response to abject suffering rather than inspired by God. On her behalf her old friend Father Van Exem has defended her saying, "In articles, books they have represented Mother Teresa as one who went round and saw the great poverty of the slums in Calcutta and her heart went out to the poor and she said 'I must do something for them'. It isn't that! The origin came from the call of Jesus."

This ability to trust and obey the call of God has characterized Mother Teresa throughout her life. Not even the thought of death has made her waver from this fundamental faith in God. When asked about the future of the Order after her death she said simply, "Let me die first, then God will provide. He will find someone more helpless, more hopeless than I to do His work."

Her achievements have always been "His Work". When describing the difficulties experienced in starting work in Italy she said, ". . . There we were taken for gypsies . . . but soon, when the people began to understand the language that we want to reach out to them with the language of God's love, then the barriers drop and somehow it works. It's God's work."

Mother Teresa has always emphasized this sense of helplessness and inadequacy. When writing to a Priest Co-Worker she wrote, "It is not how much we really have to give – but how empty we are – so that we can receive fully in our life and let Him live His life in us." One of her Sisters has also reported, "Mother says, 'If she knew what lay ahead when God called her, she would have hesitated.'"

On another occasion Mother Teresa wrote, "Put yourself completely under the influence of Jesus, so that you may think His thoughts in your mind, do His work through your hands, for you will be all-powerful with Him who strengthens you."

Such humility and a lack of self-centredness might tempt some people to imagine Mother Teresa is superhuman. The reality is rather different. Those close to her are very aware of her humanity. Some Co-Workers have wondered about the speed with which she makes some decisions, and have questioned her tendency to make a decision without hearing both sides of an issue. Evidently she is also very reluctant to change her mind about a subject, even if there are doubts about the wisdom of the situation.

People expect her to have boundless energy, but in recent years she has been seen with red-rimmed eyes and straining to raise her voice above a whisper because of exhaustion.

She has never denied that she has natural longings common to many. When a reporter asked her if she ever wanted children of her own she admitted. "Naturally, naturally. That is the sacrifice." She has also said publicly "I can make mistakes," adding, "but God does not make mistakes."

There were some in the early days who thought her plan to start a new Order was a mistake. When a senior churchman first heard about her desire to head an Order working among the poor he had some grave reservations. He protested against her request saying, "I know Mother Teresa . I knew her when she was a novice in Darjeeling . . . She couldn't even light the candles!"

Such a remark might offend long-standing supporters of Mother Teresa but she has never been one to take herself too seriously. Nothing is ever beneath her. Sitting cross-legged on the carpet in an international airport lounge, sleeping in train luggage racks or cleaning out toilets, Mother Teresa has never been one to stand on ceremony. The day she received the Nobel Peace Prize she wore her usual sari and a threadbare handknitted grey cardigan that was second-hand when she first received it.

She often did unexpected things. When meeting Queen Elizabeth II she asked after her grandchildren, and gave Prime Minister Margaret Thatcher an inexpensive plastic statue of Mary and baby Jesus. She has also been known to reduce people to helpless laugher with her jokes.

One particular favourite concerned a traveller whose car broke down at the edge of a lonely, desolate area. The only place of safety was a monastery, and the only transport the monks could offer the man was a donkey. The monks explained that to handle the animal the man must remember to say, "Amen, Amen", when he wanted it to stop, but "Thank God, thank God" when he wanted it to go forward. The journey went well until the man reached an enormous precipice. The man remembered just in time to shout "Amen, Amen". The donkey stopped inches away from the edge. Greatly relieved the man cried out, "Thank God, thank God", and over they plunged. The joke never failed to raise the spirits of her Sisters or Co-Workers.

Much to the surprise of those who are close to her, she has also been known to break her own rules. Her lifelong supporter Michael Gomes recalled, "One day, while we were talking in the courtyard of the Mother House, the bell rang and Mother herself opened the door. There was a man outside and he was very hungry, he said. 'I've told you repeatedly to go to our Children's Home next door,' Mother said, 'that's the place where we feed people.' But the man just stood there looking at Mother, and then he said very quietly that he had eaten nothing for the last two days. There is a strict rule that the Sisters are not allowed to give anything from the Mother House, not even food, but Mother just went to the kitchen, brought a plateful of food and gave it to the man. He asked if he should empty it into a cloth and take it away or should he finish it there and give back the plate. 'Take the plate and all', said Mother. The doorkeeper, Sister Antoni, was surprised out of her wits, but Mother just laughed."

Unpredictable, determined, compassionate, selfless, trusting, humble. A woman of integrity, conviction and energy. A woman who stands out in a materialistic world as someone uncorrupted by money.

Mother Teresa is all these things, yet one characteristic shines out above the others – compassion. In both the rich and poor nations of the world her name is inseparably linked with compassion. Following in the footsteps of Jesus, Mother Teresa looks "on the crowds, hungry and helpless like sheep without a Shepherd" and has compassion on them.

She is indeed a remarkable woman who can inspire us all to respond positively to the tragedies and injustices experienced by those around us. As she has said, "We, ourselves, feel that what we are doing is a drop in the ocean. But if that drop was not in the ocean then I think the ocean would be less because of that drop." There are thousands around the world who would echo those sentiments.

For further information on supporting the work of Mother Teresa and the Missionaries of Charity, please write to:

> The Co-Workers of Mother Teresa,
> Hon. Secretary,
> Mrs W. Noble,
> ''Fernhurst'',
> West Road,
> St George's Hill,
> Weybridge,
> Surrey KT13 0LZ
> England